Utah Bucket List Adventure Guide

Explore 100 Offbeat Destinations You Must Visit!

Erika Davidson

Canyon Press
canyon@purplelink.org

Please consider writing a review!
Just visit: purplelink.org/review

Copyright 2022. Canyon Press. All Rights Reserved.
No part of this book may be reproduced or transmitted in any form or by any means, electronic or mechanical, including photocopying, recording or by any other form without written permission from the publisher.

ISBN: 978-1-957590-15-8

FREE BONUS

Discover 31 Incredible Places You Can Visit Next! Just Go To:

purplelink.org/travel

Table of Contents:

How to Use This Book 1
About Utah 3
    Landscape and Climate 4

Blanding
    Bears Ears National Monument 7
    Natural Bridges National Monument 8

Bryce
    Bryce Canyon National Park 9
    Fairyland Loop 10
    Peekaboo and Spooky Slot Canyon Loop 11

Bullfrog
    Glen Canyon Recreation Area 12
    Lake Powell 13

Cedar City
    Cedar Breaks National Monument 14
    Navajo Lake 15

Delta
    Baker Hot Springs 16

Duchesne
    Starvation Reservoir 17

Escalante
    Calf Creek Falls 18
    Coyote Gulch 19
    Lower Calf Creek Falls 20

Flaming Gorge
    Flaming Gorge Reservoir 21

Fruitland
    Strawberry Reservoir 22

Garden City
    Bear Lake 23

    Conestoga Glamping Ranch 24

    Tony Grove Lake 25

Green River
    Goblin Valley State Park 26

Huntington
    Huntington State Park 27

Hurricane
    Quail Creek State Park 28

    Sand Hollow State Park 29

    Yant Flats 30

Kamas
    Mirror Lake 31

Kanab
    Coral Pink Sand Dunes 32

    Grand Staircase-Escalante National Monument 33

    Reflection Canyon 34

Kanarraville
    Kanarra Falls 35

Koosharem
    Fish Lake 36

Mexican Hat
    Monument Valley 37

    Rainbow Bridge National Monument 38

Midway
- Homestead Crater 39
- Ice Castles 40
- Memorial Hill 41
- Rocky Mountain Outfitters 42
- Soldier Hollow Nordic Center 43
- Wasatch Mountain State Park 44

Moab
- Arches National Park 45
- Balanced Rock 46
- Bartlett Wash 47
- Birthing Rock Petroglyphs 48
- Canyonlands National Park 49
- Chesler Park Loop/Joint Trail 50
- Colorado River 51
- Corona Arch 52
- Dead Horse Point State Park 53
- Delicate Arch 54
- Devils Garden Trails 55
- Double Arch 56
- Faux Waterfalls 57
- Fiery Furnace 58
- Ken's Lake 59
- Mesa Arch 60
- Needles Overlook 61
- Sand Flats Recreation Area 62

Shafer Trail Road	63
Slickrock Trail	64
Thelma & Louise Point	65
Windows Trail	66

Monticello
Newspaper Rock	67

Monroe
Mystic Hot Springs	68

Ogden
25th Street Historic District	69
Dinosaur Park and Museum	70
Great Salt Lake & Antelope Island	71
Hill Aerospace Museum	72
Waterfall Canyon	73

Orderville
Zion Ponderosa Ranch Resort	74

Panguitch
Red Canyon	75

Park City
Egyptian Theatre	76
Guardsman Pass Scenic Backway	77
Historic Main Street	78
Jordanelle Reservoir	79
Kimball Art Center	80
Park City Museum	81
Utah Olympic Park	82

Provo

Alpine Loop Scenic Byway 83
BYU Museum of Paleontology 84
Diamond Fork Hot Springs 85
Museum of Peoples and Cultures 86
Provo Beach 87
Provo Canyon Adventures 88
Provo Canyon Scenic Byway 89
Provo Pioneer Village 90
Provo River Parkway Trail 91
Splash Summit Waterpark 92
The Covey Center for the Arts 93
Utah Lake State Park 94

Salt Lake City
American Fork Canyon 95
Beehive House 96
Blackridge Reservoir 97
Bridger Bay Beach 98
City Creek Center 99
Hogle Zoo 100
Joseph Smith Memorial Building 101
Liberty Park 102
Mormon Tabernacle 103
Mormon Temple 104
Natural History Museum of Utah 105
Salt Lake City Canyons 106
Temple Square 107

This is the Place Heritage Park.................................. 108

Timpanogos Cave National Monument................... 109

Tracy Aviary... 110

Utah State Capitol.. 111

Springdale
Angels Landing 112

Grafton Ghost Town... 113

The Narrows 114

Zion National Park 115

St. George
Snow Canyon State Park 116

St. George 117

Torrey
Capitol Reef National Park...................................... 118

Vernal
Dinosaur National Monument 119

Red Fleet State Park 120

Uinta Mountains and Mirror Lake Highway 121

Wendover
Bonneville Salt Flats.. 122

Willard
Willard Bay 123

Proper Planning.. 125

How to Use This Book

Welcome to your very own adventure guide to exploring the many wonders of the state of Utah. Not only does this book offer the most wonderful places to visit and sights to see in the vast state, but it provides GPS coordinates for Google Maps to make exploring that much easier.

Adventure Guide
Sorted by region, this guide offers over 100 amazing wonders found in Utah for you to see and explore. They can be visited in any order and this book will help you keep track of where you've been and where to look forward to going next. Each section describes the area or place, what to look for, Physical Address, and what you may need to bring along.

GPS Coordinates
As you can imagine, not all of the locations in this book have a physical address. Fortunately, some of our listed wonders are either located within a National Park or Reserve, or near a city, town, or place of business. For those that are not associated with a specific location, it is easiest to map it using GPS coordinates.

Luckily, Google has a system of codes that converts the coordinates into pin-drop locations that Google Maps can interpret and navigate.

Each adventure in this guide includes GPS coordinates along with a physical address whenever it is available.

It is important that you are prepared for poor cell signals. It is recommended that you route your location and ensure that the directions are accessible offline. Depending on your device and the distance of some locations, you may need to travel with a backup battery source.

About Utah

Utah became the 45th American state on January 4, 1896. The state's name is derived from the Ute tribe, which means "people of the mountains." Indigenous people have lived in the area for centuries, with archaeological evidence dating back 10,000 years.

Because the land that is now Utah was once a swamp in which they roamed, it is one of the best states to find dinosaur fossils. At over 23 feet long, the world's largest raptor lived in Utah and became known as the "Utahraptor."

Encompassing 84,900 square miles, Utah is the 11th largest state in the U.S. in terms of land. It is also one of the "Four Corners" states, along with Arizona, Colorado, and New Mexico. Together, these four states meet at a single point; the only place this occurs in the entire country.

Utah is also a cultural center for Mormonism, with Mormons accounting for around 60% of the state's population. Before it was named Utah, the region was known as the "State of Deseret," which means *honey* in the Book of Mormon. The Beehive State's motto is "industry" because of the industrious nature of the honeybee.

This symbol and motto are included on the state flag of Utah. Major industries such as coal mining, salt production, cattle ranching, and government services are a part of Utah's growing economy.

Utah is also home to five national parks, seven national monuments, and two National Recreation Areas. It is a gorgeous state full of magnificent landscapes to explore and year-round recreational activities to enjoy.

Landscape and Climate

Most of Utah's landscape consists of mountains, high plateaus, and deserts. The state contains part of three major geographical areas: the Rocky Mountains, the Basin and Ridge Region, and the Colorado Plateau. On average, the peaks in Utah are the tallest in the country, with King's Peak at the highest point of 13,528 feet.

There are also miles of salt flats as far as the eye can see. These vast areas make it possible to race cars at record-breaking speeds. Drivers can speed for miles without worrying about any obstacles. However, years of this activity have thinned the salt crust substantially.

The western part of the state is a mostly arid desert with small mountain ranges and rugged terrain, while the southern landscape features mesmerizing canyons, mesas, arches, buttes, and gullies. Eastern Utah is full of high-elevation basins and plateaus. The Great Salt Lake is in northern Utah. It's the largest saltwater lake in the Western Hemisphere.

Utah is one of the driest states with low humidity percentages second only to Nevada. On average, Utah enjoys 300 sunny days per year. The summers are long and scorching hot, and average high temperatures range from 85°F to 100°F in July. Temperatures drop dramatically at night, however, and are cool and pleasant.

Winters are short and cold. At the peak of the cold season, temperatures are between 30°F to 55°F.

The mountains near Salt Lake City receive an average of 500 inches of snow per year, which makes for some of the best skiing conditions in the country. In fact, Utah's license plate claims that the state has "the greatest snow on Earth." This is attributed to not only the amount but also the perfect balance of wetness versus fluffiness with a snow density of 8.5 percent.

Bears Ears National Monument

Bears Ears was designated as a national monument rather recently in 2016. The pair of towering buttes is distinctive against the scenery of its surroundings. The park is divided into two units named Indian Creek and Shash Jaa, and the entire area features expanses of red rock, high plateaus, juniper forests, and a legacy of Native cultures. You can hike, visit cultural sites, mountain bike, float on the river, and ride off-highway vehicles. The land of the monument contains many artifacts and archaeological sites that are historical and sacred. Visitors are urged to learn how to protect the monument before exploring.

Best Time to Visit: Visit during the spring or fall.

Pass/Permit/Fees: There is no fee to visit Bears Ears National Monument. However, some hiking and camping areas have fees and a permit required for overnight backpacking at a rate of $8 per person per trip.

Closest City or Town: Blanding, Utah

Physical Address:
365 N. Main Street
Monticello, UT 84535

GPS Coordinates: 37.62916° N, 109.86790° W

Did You Know? Bears Ears was the first national monument ever designated at the request of Indigenous tribes. It's one of the most extensive archaeological areas on Earth.

Natural Bridges National Monument

Featuring the thirteenth-largest natural bridge in the world, along with several others, Natural Bridges National Monument was formed when water flowed through the stream bed of the canyon over millions of years. During flash floods, the water undercut the walls of rock to create bridges. Eventually, as a bridge's opening gets larger, erosion and gravity will combine to collapse it. As the Owachomo Natural Bridge has a very large opening, it's possible it might not stand much longer. Native Americans have lived in the area since 7500 BCE, with Europeans first visiting the area in 1883.

Best Time to Visit: The best time to visit is late October through November, as this is when the monarch butterflies are in the area.

Pass/Permit/Fees: There is a $20 fee per vehicle to visit Natural Bridges Natural Monument.

Closest City or Town: Blanding, Utah

Physical Address:
Blanding Visitor's Center
12 N. Grayson Parkway
Blanding, UT 84511

GPS Coordinates: 37.60470° N, 110.00520° W

Did You Know? Natural Bridges National Monument was the first designated International Dark Sky Park, which means it is protected because it has no light pollution.

Bryce Canyon National Park

Famous for its unique geology, Bryce Canyon features colorful limestone rocks in red, orange, and white. The park contains thousands of spire-shaped rock formations called *hoodoos* that can reach up to 200 feet high. The expansive Bryce Amphitheater is part of a series of amphitheaters that extend more than 20 miles within the park. The Rim Trail is the most traveled, but there are other branching trails along the way to explore. Visitors can also drive through and stop at notable overlooks like Sunrise Point, Sunset Point, Bryce Point, and Inspiration Point. Hiking is always an option, with snowshoeing or skiing in the winter. There are trails for every skill level. Horseback riding and camping are also available. The park is designated as an International Dark Sky Park.

Best Time to Visit: The best time to visit Bryce Canyon National Park is between May and September.

Pass/Permit/Fees: A 7-day pass is $35 for vehicles, $30 for motorcycles, or $20 per person.

Closest City or Town: Bryce, Utah

Physical Address:
Bryce Canyon County Visitor Center
755 W. Main Street
Escalante, UT 84726

GPS Coordinates: 37.5930° N, 112.1871° W

Did You Know? There is a hoodoo in Bryce Canyon National Park called Thor's Hammer because of its unique shape.

Fairyland Loop

Beginning at Fairyland Point in Bryce Canyon National Park, the Fairyland Loop is a hiking trail that takes visitors past hoodoos, along the canyon rim, and down into the canyon. The 8-mile round-trip hike is rated as strenuous because of the length and multiple elevation changes. On the way to the canyon bottom, visitors will see multi-colored stone, towering rock spires, and winding labyrinthian paths. The loop descends to the base of Boat Mesa before returning back to Fairyland Point. Be sure to stop for the Tower Bridge, a large hoodoo that is surrounded by two natural arches and the China Wall, a grouping of multiple hoodoos set atop a small ridge.

Best Time to Visit: Hike Fairyland Loop is in the spring or fall because the heat is less intense.

Pass/Permit/Fees: There is a $35 fee per vehicle, per week to visit Bryce Canyon National Park.

Closest City or Town: Bryce, Utah

Physical Address:
Escalante Interagency Visitor Center
755 W. Main Street
Escalante, UT 84726

GPS Coordinates: 37.65051° N, 112.14744° W

Did You Know? If you're a photographer hoping to get pictures of a spectacular sunrise, hike the Fairyland Loop counterclockwise starting at dawn.

Peekaboo and Spooky Slot Canyon Loop

A family favorite in the Dry Fork part of the Grand Staircase-Escalante area, Spooky Gulch is famous for how dark and narrow it gets inside. Nearby Peekaboo Gulch is full of beautiful sandstone arches. These canyons are a scenic vista of red and purple rock, and the natural contours and waves of the sandstone are awe-inspiring. There is some tame climbing and rock scrambling involved, so it is a moderately difficult trek. These adventures can be done individually, but they pair perfectly in a loop that you can tackle in one afternoon. The recommended route is to take Peekaboo Gulch first, which takes you north. Upon exiting, hike overland to the east for half a mile until you reach Spooky Gulch. The entire loop is about 3 miles and takes most hikers around 3 to 4 hours.

Best Time to Visit: Visit in the spring or fall.

Pass/Permit/Fees: There is no fee to visit.

Closest City or Town: Bryce, Utah

Physical Address:
Bryce Canyon County Visitor Center
755 W. Main Street
Escalante, UT 84726

GPS Coordinates: 37.4814° N, 111.2166° W

Did You Know? Spooky Gulch is only ten inches wide in some spots.

Glen Canyon Recreation Area

Glen Canyon is a natural canyon that was carved by the Colorado River. Hundreds of miles of scenic vistas and geological wonders can be found in this rugged, high-desert terrain. Glen Canyon Recreation Area encompasses the area around Lake Powell, which lies between the states of Utah and Arizona. It features water-based and backcountry recreational activities. Opportunities for fishing, boating, swimming, hiking, kayaking, and four-wheel driving on off-roading trails are available throughout the park. The hike to Horseshoe Bend is one of the most popular day hikes. There are also several routes for scenic drives, such as the Burr Trail and Hole-in-the-Rock Road.

Best Time to Visit: The best time to visit is in the fall.

Pass/Permit/Fees: There is an entry fee of $30 per vehicle, $25 per motorcycle, $15 per individual, or $30 per boat/vessel to visit Glen Canyon Recreation Area, all valid for 7 days.

Closest City or Town: Bullfrog, Utah

Physical Address:
Escalante Interagency Visitor Center
755 W. Main Street
Escalante, UT 84726

GPS Coordinates: 41.3724° N, 112.2026° W

Did You Know? Glen Canyon Recreation Area begins at the Grand Canyon in Lees Ferry, Arizona and stretches to the Orange Cliffs of Utah.

Lake Powell

Lake Powell is one of the most popular places in the country for boating, water skiing, camping, hiking, fishing, and exploring the Glen Canyon National Recreation Area. Three million people visit this second-largest man-made lake in the U.S. every year to swim and boat in the clear blue waters or camp and hike on the surrounding sandstone. Lake Powell was created in 1963 when the Glen Canyon Dam was built on the Arizona side of the lake. It was constructed to regulate water availability to Utah, Colorado, Arizona, New Mexico, California, Nevada, and Wyoming through the Colorado River Compact.

Best Time to Visit: The best time to visit Lake Powell is between May and August.

Pass/Permit/Fees: There is a $30 fee per vehicle to visit Lake Powell. The pass is valid for 7 days.

Closest City or Town: Bullfrog, Utah

Physical Address:
Escalante Interagency Visitor Center
755 W. Main Street
Escalante, UT 84726

GPS Coordinates: 37.16293° N, 111.23883° W

Did You Know? Lake Powell is named for Major John Wesley Powell, who led an 1869 expedition into what is now known as Glen Canyon National Recreation Area.

Cedar Breaks National Monument

A natural amphitheater with a rim over 10,000 feet above sea level, Cedar Breaks stretches across 3 miles with a depth of over 2,000 feet. The canyon was formed from erosion and uplift over millions of years. Much of the area at the top is covered in volcanic rock, and the muted rainbow colors offer amazing scenery. There are a variety of hiking trails to explore, many of which are ranked as easy to moderate. Sunset Trail runs between two overlooks; Nature Trail is great for wildlife viewing. Alpine Pond Loop Trail forms a figure eight through forests and meadows, and South Rim Trail offers spectacular views. Trails start at over 10,000 feet in elevation, so it's best to get acclimated first.

Best Time to Visit: Visit between June and October.

Pass/Permit/Fees: There is a $10 entry fee to visit Cedar Breaks National Monument that is good for 7 days.

Closest City or Town: Cedar City, Utah

Physical Address:
Cedar Breaks National Monument Visitor Contact Station
4730 UT-148
Brain Head, UT 84719

GPS Coordinates: 37.6347° N, 112.8451° W

Did You Know? The park is situated in one of the largest regions of natural darkness in the lower 48 states, offering opportunities for astrotourism.

Navajo Lake

Located in the Dixie National Forest, Navajo lake is a small reservoir in Kane County of southern Utah. The lake also has a naturally occurring dam on the eastern side of the valley. The area is host to various lodging facilities, fishing, and boating activities, despite the lake only being about 25 feet deep. Ancient lava beds surround the area, including Mammoth Cave, which can be explored. There are signs that direct travelers to the site. You can also mountain bike a 12-mile trail around the lake called the Navajo Lake Loop Trail while catching some great views along the way. There is even a 1-mile hiking trail to the nearby Cascade Falls. Camping is available at the Navajo Lake Campground.

Best Time to Visit: It is excellent to visit year-round.

Pass/Permit/Fees: There is no fee to visit Navajo Lake. For camping, the daily fee is $10 for walk-in tents, $12 for a single site, or $20 for a double site. The maximum stay permitted is 14 days.

Closest City or Town: Cedar City, Utah

Physical Address:
Navajo Lake Campground
820 N. Main Street
Cedar City, UT 84720

GPS Coordinates: 37.5233° N, 112.7783° W

Did You Know? Originally known as Cloud Lake to the Paiutes, Navajo Lake was formed by lava flow many years ago.

Baker Hot Springs

Baker Hot Springs is a more rustic, less frequented spring to visit. This remote location features small natural hot springs surrounded by a vast desert landscape. There are three concrete soaking tubs that can accommodate several people. A neat feature is the trench system, which brings hot water in on one side and cool water from the other. The cool water is sourced from another natural spring in the area. You can alter the flow of each to control the temperature of the water. Also known as Crater Springs and Abraham Hot Springs, these springs are accessible by car. Be aware of road conditions because the location is a bit off the beaten path. Camping is permitted in the area.

Best Time to Visit: The best time to visit Baker Hot Springs is in the winter, spring, or fall.

Pass/Permit/Fees: There is no fee to visit Baker Hot Springs.

Closest City or Town: Delta, Utah

Physical Address:
Millard County Visitor's Center
75 W. Main Street
Delta, UT 84624

GPS Coordinates: 39.6127° N, 112.7291° W

Did You Know? The Baker Hot Springs are heated by the volcanic activity of Fumarole Butte.

Starvation Reservoir

Found inside the Fred Hayes State Park, Starvation Reservoir is secluded and full of natural diversity. The water is a beautiful turquoise, and the reservoir is stocked with fish every season. There are recreational activities of all kinds, including boating, skiing, paddleboarding, and fishing. You can hike or check out the off-roading trails. There's even an archery course where you can use your own equipment or borrow some from the park. There are also developed and primitive campgrounds to stay overnight at this reservoir in the desert.

Best Time to Visit: The best time to visit Starvation Reservoir is between May and September.

Pass/Permit/Fees: There is a $10 day-use fee to visit Starvation Reservoir.

Closest City or Town: Duchesne, Utah

Physical Address:
24220 W. 7655 South State Park Road
Duchesne, UT 84021

GPS Coordinates: 40.1868° N, 110.4674° W

Did You Know? There are several different legends tied to the naming of Starvation Reservoir. All the stories end with starvation caused by the harsh, hostile environment of the late 1800s and early 1900s.

Calf Creek Falls

The Grand Staircase-Escalante National Monument is protected land in southern Utah that holds historical and scientific significance. A perennial stream called Calf Creek is located within the area. There are also two waterfalls that you can visit for a desert-oasis experience. The upper falls are 88 feet high and require a very steep trail to access. The trail is difficult to navigate in some areas, so most people opt for the easier route to the lower falls. The lower falls hike has a bigger drop and is the more popular of the two. It is a 6-mile round-trip hike that is relatively flat. The waterfall is 126 feet and streams down along the mineral-stained sandstone. A pool at the base is great for swimming and cooling off in the summer.

Best Time to Visit: The best time to visit Calf Creek Falls is between spring and fall, mid-week to avoid crowds.

Pass/Permit/Fees: There is a $5 fee per vehicle to visit Calf Creek Falls.

Closest City or Town: Escalante, Utah

Physical Address:
Bryce Canyon County Visitor Center
755 W. Main
Escalante, UT 84726

GPS Coordinates: 37.8292° N, 111.4201° W

Did You Know? The creek was used as a natural pen for calves in the late 1800s and early 1900s.

Coyote Gulch

Coyote Gulch is a winding, semi-narrow canyon located in the Grand Staircase-Escalante desert. Expect to see arches, wetlands, domes, waterfalls, and a natural bridge set within red-rock country. One of the more popular routes is through Crack-in-the-Rock, but there are several options for accessing the gulch. The "Sneaker Route" is the most direct and can be traveled within a day. The latter requires rope for the descent into the gulch. At up to 26 miles, the entire canyon adventure is well suited for an overnight camp, especially since you will definitely want to explore as you go. You can customize your route to be shorter as needed. Either way, be prepared for some serious navigation and rock scrambling.

Best Time to Visit: The best time to visit Coyote Gulch is in the spring or fall.

Pass/Permit/Fees: There is no fee to visit Coyote Gulch, but a free permit is required for camping or backpacking.

Closest City or Town: Escalante, Utah

Physical Address:
Bryce Canyon County Visitor Center
755 W. Main Street
Escalante, UT 84726

GPS Coordinates: 37.4279° N, 110.9809° W

Did You Know? Stevens Arch is one of the largest arches in the U.S. It can be found northeast of the Escalante-Coyote Gulch confluence.

Lower Calf Creek Falls

Lower Calf Creek Falls is a 130-foot waterfall located in the Grand Staircase-Escalante National Monument. It features a deep swimming hole and is surrounded by lush, green vegetation and multi-colored striated sandstone. Of the two waterfalls on Calf Creek, the lower one is the most popular and, since the formation of the national monument in the 1990s, has seen an increase in visitors each year. There is a 3-mile hike (one way) to the waterfall, but it is rated as easy because it is mostly flat and well marked. Even on the hottest days of summer, the cool water flowing over the cliff gives off a refreshing mist, keeping swimmers comfortable. Along the path to the waterfall, visitors will pass beaver dams, two granaries, and a pictograph on wall across from the canyon.

Best Time to Visit: Visit in the spring and summer after a rainstorm, when the falls are at their fullest.

Pass/Permit/Fees: There is no fee to visit.

Closest City or Town: Escalante, Utah

Physical Address:
Escalante Interagency Visitor Center
755 W. Main Street
Escalante, UT 84726

GPS Coordinates: 37.82997° N, 111.42020° W

Did You Know? Calf Creek is named for the time when the area was used as a natural calf pen in the late 1800s and early 1900s.

Flaming Gorge Reservoir

Surrounded by the beautiful red-rock mountains, this 91-mile-long reservoir was formed by damming the Green River. Featuring outstanding opportunities for water sports like boating, fishing, parasailing, rafting, or jet skiing, the Flaming Gorge Reservoir is shared between southwest Wyoming and northeastern Utah. There are three full-service marinas for launching, storing, and maintaining your vessels. At an elevation of 6,040 feet, the temperatures are moderate at around 80°F during the summer months. The reservoir provides an excellent habitat for fish and is famous for its trophy lake fish.

Best Time to Visit: The best time to visit Flaming Gorge Reservoir is in the spring or summer.

Pass/Permit/Fees: There is no fee to visit Flaming Gorge Reservoir, but a Recreation Use Pass is required at all major boat launches and the Little National Recreation Trail below the dam. It costs $5 per day, $15 for 16 days, or $35 for an annual pass.

Closest City or Town: Flaming Gorge, Utah

Physical Address:
25 UT-43
Manila, UT 84046

GPS Coordinates: 41.0917° N, 109.5390° W

Did You Know? The name Flaming Gorge was inspired by the sun reflecting off the bright red rocks around the Green and Colorado rivers.

Strawberry Reservoir

Located near the Uinta National Forest of the Watch Mountains, Strawberry Reservoir sits in an open mountain valley and is best known for its fishing. As Utah's most popular fishery, more than 1.5 million angling hours are put in at Strawberry Reservoir per year. There are four major fishing zones in the area, including Strawberry Basin, Meadows Basin, Soldier Creek Basin, and the Narrows. Large rainbow trout, cutthroat trout, and kokanee salmon are a few sought-after catches. There are regulations in place regarding the possession, release, and quantity allowed of certain species of fish. Aside from fishing, there are also various trails to explore in the area, and camping is available around the reservoir.

Best Time to Visit: Strawberry Reservoir is excellent to visit any time of year, even for ice fishing in the winter.

Pass/Permit/Fees: A 3-day license to fish at Strawberry Reservoir costs $28 for nonresidents and $16 for residents. There is also a $55 fee for a weekly boat launch pass if you plan to fish on the lake.

Closest City or Town: Fruitland, Utah

Physical Address:
1555 Strawberry Bay Road
Heber City, UT 84032

GPS Coordinates: 40.1718° N, 111.1295° W

Did You Know? Currently, the state record for the largest cutthroat trout caught was set at this location in 1930 with a 27-pound fish.

Bear Lake

Formed 28,000 years ago by earthquake activity, Bear Lake is 20 miles long, 8 miles wide, and 208 feet deep. It is full of natural fresh water and split equally between the states of Utah and Idaho at an elevation of 5,924 feet. The lake has been nicknamed the "Caribbean of the Rockies" for the beautiful turquoise color caused by the calcium carbonate suspended in the lake's waters. Fishing, swimming, skiing, camping, and hiking are popular activities in the area, depending on the season. The lake sits in the middle of the valley, surrounded by mountains. It includes the State Marina and Rendezvous Beach on Utah's side. The park's East Side area consists of Cisco Beach, South Eden, North Eden, Rainbow Cove, and First Point.

Best Time to Visit: Visit Bear Lake any time of year, depending on recreational interests.

Pass/Permit/Fees: There is a $15 daily fee per vehicle to visit Bear Lake. This fee goes up to $20 on Saturdays and holidays from June through Labor Day.

Closest City or Town: Garden City, Utah

Physical Address:
Bear Lake Valley Convention and Visitors Bureau
69 N. Paradise Parkway, Building A
Garden City, UT 84028

GPS Coordinates: 42.0299° N, 111.3322° W

Did You Know? The area is regionally famous for its delicious raspberries and raspberry milkshakes.

Conestoga Glamping Ranch

Experience the glorious Utah scenery and natural wonders while camping in modern luxury at the Conestoga Glamping Ranch. No one says you have to give up the comforts of home to experience the great outdoors. By booking accommodations at this glampsite, you can experience nature from a cozy tent, complete with comfy beds, luxury linens, electricity, and more. You have the choice of Royal or Grand Tents that sleep between two and six people, covered wagon cabins that sleep between four and six people, or Traditional Tents that sleep four people. Royal and Grand Tents include en-suite bathrooms, mini refrigerators, private campfire patios, dining tables, and comfortable furnishings. Traditional Tents have heaters, private campfire patios, dining tables, and Adirondack chairs.

Best Time to Visit: The best time to visit the Conestoga Glamping Ranch is between May and September.

Pass/Permit/Fees: The fee to visit Conestoga Glamping Ranch depends on the accommodations and dates you choose. Check the website for pricing information.

Closest City or Town: Garden City, Utah

Physical Address:
427 N. Paradise Parkway
Garden City, UT 84028

GPS Coordinates: 41.95422° N, 111.40267° W

Did You Know? Wagons are fully mobile and can be moved for customized experiences.

Tony Grove Lake

Tony Grove, a glacial lake located in the Uinta-Wasatch-Cache National Forest, is augmented by the use of a dam built in the 1930s. Featuring an assortment of summer wildflowers and excellent trails, this location is designated a U.S. Forest Service Wildflower Viewing Area. There is an easy trail that circles the lake, and there are additional trails that take you into the Mt. Naomi Wilderness or up to White Pike Lake. Visitors come for fishing, canoeing, paddleboarding, and to enjoy the fresh mountain air. Primitive camping is available at the Tony Grove Lake Campground, and reservations are recommended. There is also primitive wilderness camping in the Mt. Naomi Wilderness area.

Best Time to Visit: The best time to visit is between July and August for peak flower viewing.

Pass/Permit/Fees: There is a daily entry fee of $6 per car to visit Tony Grove Lake. Visitors can also purchase a 7-day pass for $20 or a full-summer pass for $35.

Closest City or Town: Garden City, Utah

Physical Address:
Cache Valley Visitors Bureau and Gift Shop
199 Main Street
Logan, UT 84321

GPS Coordinates: 41.8927° N, 111.6430° W

Did You Know? The name of the lake is derived from its popularity with wealthy residents of Logan in the late 19th and early 20th centuries.

Goblin Valley State Park

A showcase of geologic history that started around 170 million years ago, this park was once a vast sea. The inland sea deposited layers of sand, mud, and silt that were sculpted by erosion and wind over time. The park features hundreds of hoodoos. These mushroom-shaped rock pinnacles are locally referred to as "goblins," and the landscape is often compared to the surface of the planet Mars.

The area is surrounded by a wall of eroded cliffs to complete the colorful landscape. You can do some sightseeing from the park overlook and hike among the fun-shaped goblins on and off the trail. Visitors come to explore, take photos, and view the wildlife.

Best Time to Visit: The best times to visit Goblin Valley State Park are in the spring and fall.

Pass/Permit/Fees: There is a $13 daily fee per vehicle to visit Goblin Valley State Park.

Closest City or Town: Green River, Utah

Physical Address:
18630 Goblin Valley Road
Green River, UT 84525

GPS Coordinates: 38.5737° N, 110.7071° W

Did You Know? The movie *Galaxy Quest* was filmed at Goblin Valley.

Huntington State Park

This beautiful setting features crimson buttes coupled with the evergreen colors of pinyon and juniper trees. A quiet desert oasis surrounded by sandstone cliffs and peaks, this scenic place is a perfect spot to come and relax. The sea-colored, warm-water reservoir is great for water skiing, boating, and fishing. The Outback Nature Trail takes you around the reservoir for a 2.7-mile wildlife adventure. There are 25 campsites and numerous picnic sites, so it's suitable for a day or overnight trip.

Best Time to Visit: Huntington State Park is great to visit any time of year.

Pass/Permit/Fees: There is a $10 day-use fee to visit Huntington State Park. Use of the watercraft launches is included.

Closest City or Town: Huntington, Utah

Physical Address:
Stuart Guard Station Visitor Center
FR0110
Huntington, UT 84528

GPS Coordinates: 39.3481° N, 110.9436° W

Did You Know? The town and the reservoir were named in honor of the three Huntington Brothers who first explored the area in 1855.

Quail Creek State Park

Quail Creek State Park features a great campsite and reservoir within a red-rock desert setting. The water is a clear green, surrounded by colorful cliffs and the Pine Valley Mountains. The 600-acre reservoir is formed by two dams and has a maximum depth of 120 feet. It is cold enough to sustain rainbow trout, bullhead catfish, and crappie, which are all stocked. The warmer, upper levels of water are great for the stocked largemouth bass and bluegill. The warm waters and mild winter climate make this park a year-round destination. Visitors come to boat, camp, fish, and swim. There are 23 single-family campsites to choose from around the reservoir.

Best Time to Visit: Quail Creek State Park is excellent to visit any time of the year.

Pass/Permit/Fees: There is $15 day-use fee to visit Quail Creek State Park. Use of the boat ramp is included.

Closest City or Town: Hurricane, Utah

Physical Address:
472 N. 5300 West
Hurricane, UT 84737

GPS Coordinates: 37.1879° N, 113.3941° W

Did You Know? The reservoir was completed in 1985 to provide culinary water and irrigation to the nearby St. George area.

Sand Hollow State Park

Picture warm blue waters against a red-rock landscape and red-sand beaches. The reservoir is a great place for water sports, fishing, boating, and swimming. There is also plenty to explore around the shores. The north side is full of slickrock, while the south offers sandy beaches.

One of Utah's newer state parks, Sand Hollow features 15,000 acres of pristine sand dunes. There are several off-roading trails so that you can explore the dunes of Sand Mountain. There are even three campgrounds to choose from if you'd rather plan for multi-day adventures. You can drive your ATV from the Sandpit Campground right to the dunes and back for extra fun and convenience.

Best Time to Visit: The best time to visit Sand Hollow State Park is between May and September.

Pass/Permit/Fees: There is a $15 fee per vehicle to visit Sand Hollow State Park.

Closest City or Town: Hurricane, Utah

Physical Address:
3351 Sand Hollow Road
Hurricane, UT 84737

GPS Coordinates: 37.1200° N, 113.3820° W

Did You Know? The reservoir is 1,322 acres, but the entire park occupies 20,000 acres.

Yant Flats

Not a widely known location, Yant Flats is the southern boundary of a rocky plateau that is richly colored in shades of orange, pink, red, yellow, and white. The Yant Flats trail leads across the southern slopes of the Pine Valley Mountains. It is 3.4 miles round trip on a trail that is rated moderate. Over time, the sandstone layers at the edge of the Colorado Plateau have been pushed up by an underlying volcanic rock. After being exposed, they've eroded into domes, cliffs, and canyons. The layers of rock and their colors have created an incredible marbled effect with remarkably colored sandstone formations.

Best Time to Visit: The best time to visit Yant Flats is in the spring or fall.

Pass/Permit/Fees: There is no fee to visit Yant Flats.

Closest City or Town: Hurricane, Utah

Physical Address:
Happy Trails Adventure Tours
291 N. Main Street
Leeds, UT 84746

GPS Coordinates: 37.2300° N, 113.4683° W

Did You Know? The cliffs in the area are so colorful that they are called the "candy cliffs of Utah."

Mirror Lake

At an elevation of 10,400 feet, Mirror Lake is easily accessed from the Mirror Lake Scenic Byway that brings visitors up into the Uinta Mountains. A popular spot for fishing and recreation, the lake's name comes from the pristine reflection of the surrounding mountains and trees. You can take a day trip or stay overnight at the Mirror Lake Campground located on the shore. The lake is surrounded by the Uinta-Wasatch-Cache National Forest, and there is an abundance of trails to explore beyond the lake and into the wilderness.

Best Time to Visit: The best time to visit Mirror Lake is in August.

Pass/Permit/Fees: There is a day-use fee of $6 for up to 3 days or a $12 fee for up to 7 days to visit Mirror Lake. Camping fees vary.

Closest City or Town: Kamas, Utah

Physical Address:
Rock Cliff Nature Center
2500 UT-32
Kamas, UT 84036

GPS Coordinates: 40.7044° N, 110.8888° W

Did You Know? You can enjoy a spectacular view of the lake from atop Bald Mountain. The Mirror Lake Scenic Byway gets you within 1,500 feet of the summit.

Coral Pink Sand Dunes

The erosion of pink-colored Navajo sandstone from the Middle Jurassic period has created dunes of pink sand. The dunes are estimated to be 10,000–15,000 years old and are surrounded by red-sandstone cliffs. The park is at 6,000 feet in elevation. Of the 3,730 acres, 2,000 acres of sand are open to off-roading adventures. Riders can traverse Sand Highway in a small canyon and the South Boundary Trail. There aren't really any formal trails, and visitors are welcome to explore the dunes on foot too. The park also allows for camping, photography, and hiking, along with off roading.

Best Time to Visit: The best time to visit the Coral Pink Sand Dunes is in the spring or fall.

Pass/Permit/Fees: There is a $10 fee per vehicle to visit the Coral Pink Sand Dunes.

Closest City or Town: Kanab, Utah

Physical Address:
Visitor Center
745 US-89
Kanab, UT 84741

GPS Coordinates: 37.0377° N, 112.7144° W

Did You Know? Coral Pink Sand Dunes is the only place in the world where the coral pink tiger beetle is found.

Grand Staircase-Escalante National Monument

The Grand Staircase-Escalante National Monument spans nearly 1.87 million acres and five life zones, which include both low-lying desert and high-altitude coniferous forest. It originally belonged to the Anasazi and Fremont Native American tribes between 950 and 1100 CE. There are various occupation sites, granaries, and rock art panels that were left behind by these cultures, some of which are still visible today. Numerous fossils have also been found in the area, providing scientists with more valuable information about ecosystem change at the end of the dinosaur era than any other fossil site in the world.

Best Time to Visit: The best times to visit Grand Staircase-Escalante National Monument are late March through June and early September through October.

Pass/Permit/Fees: There is no fee to visit.

Closest City or Town: Kanab, Utah

Physical Address:
Visitor Center
745 US-89
Kanab, UT 84741

GPS Coordinates: 37.40504° N, 111.68447 W

Did You Know? In 2017, the land encompassing Grand Staircase-Escalante National Monument was cut in half, though it was restored in full by October 2021.

Reflection Canyon

Reflection Canyon is a part of the Glen Canyon National Recreation Area and has a stunning view. The 16- to 18-mile round-trip trail is recommended only for experienced adventurers due to its length, terrain, and difficulty to locate. The view is in a remote area and can be done in a 1-day hiking trip; however, some opt to backpack overnight to rise with the sun. You will need a vehicle with a high profile and four-wheel drive to access the trailhead via an unmaintained and unpaved route. There is no clearly marked trail, so prepare to navigate carefully.

Best Time to Visit: The best time to visit Reflection Canyon is between March and November.

Pass/Permit/Fees: There is a fee of $30 per vehicle, $25 per motorcycle, or $15 per pedestrian/bicycle to visit Reflection Canyon. A backcountry permit is also required for all overnight trips.

Closest City or Town: Kanab, Utah

Physical Address:
Visitor Center
745 US-89
Kanab, UT 84741

GPS Coordinates: 37.1883° N, 110.9184° W

Did You Know? The location of this wonder was revealed in 2006 when photographer Michael Melford's photos of the canyon were published in *National Geographic*.

Kanarra Falls

Kanarra Creek offers a slot-canyon water hike featuring waterfalls and a natural water slide. Water flows year round, so hikers must wade the stream at certain places on the trail. There are two waterfalls, with the first approximately 1.6 miles into the hike. The trip to the first waterfall is easy and short, but if you want a moderate challenge, you can climb the falls and continue into the canyon. To continue past the first waterfall, you will need to scale a lean-to log ladder with metal rungs. Further on, you will also need to climb a large boulder with no ladders or handholds. The route and length of this adventure are customizable, so you can choose to keep it easy or go for more of a challenge.

Best Time to Visit: Do not enter this canyon when flash flood warnings are in effect in the Kanarraville, Cedar Breaks, or Zion areas.

Pass/Permit/Fees: There is a $12 permit fee to visit Kanarra Falls. The hike is limited to 150 people per day.

Closest City or Town: Kanarraville, Utah

Physical Address:
Cedar City Visitor Center
581 N. Main Street
Cedar City, UT 84721

GPS Coordinates: 37.5377° N, 113.1525° W

Did You Know? These waterfalls are two of the most photographed in Utah.

Fish Lake

At an elevation of 8,848 feet, Fish Lake is a high alpine lake that lies within the Fishlake National Forest. The lake is 6 miles long and 1 mile wide. The southeast shore is bounded by the Mytoge Mountains, and the northwest shore is bounded by Fish Lake Hightop Plateau. It is the largest natural mountain lake in the state of Utah. The lake holds large mackinaw, rainbow trout, lake trout, splake, kokanee salmon, brown trout, tiger trout, and yellow perch. There are several surrounding campgrounds and three boat ramps on the west shore. Multiple trails for hiking and biking can be found in the area as well. The Lakeshore National Recreation Trail is 17 miles long and a great option for exploring by foot or bike.

Best Time to Visit: The best time to visit Fish Lake is in the summer or fall.

Pass/Permit/Fees: There is no fee to visit Fish Lake, but there is a camping fee that varies by site.

Closest City or Town: Koosharem, Utah

Physical Address:
Fishlake National Forest
575 S. Main Street
Beaver, UT 84713

GPS Coordinates: 38.5502° N, 111.7078° W

Did You Know? The world-famous Pando Aspen Clone is near the lake. It is the world's heaviest living organism at 13 million pounds.

Monument Valley

Located on the Utah–Arizona state border, Monument Valley is known for its towering sandstone buttes. These sandstone masterpieces are found along with colossal mesas and panoramic views in the Monument Valley Navajo Tribal Park. The towers reach heights of 400–1,000 feet. It is possible to drive through Monument Valley and visit the main sites within a few hours. If you really want to explore, consider spending the day. Tribal Park Loop is a 17-mile scenic drive past the most popular sites. The only self-guided tour available is the Wildcat Trail, and all other hikes must be done with a guide. There are many options for tours depending on how much time you wish to spend.

Best Time to Visit: Visit Monument Valley during the spring or fall.

Pass/Permit/Fees: There is a $20 fee per vehicle to visit Monument Valley. Tours cost around $80–$90 depending on the company, with one overnight excursion costing up to $300.

Closest City or Town: Mexican Hat, Utah

Physical Address:
Bears Ears Education Center
567 Main Street
Bluff, UT 84512

GPS Coordinates: 36.9980° N, 110.0985° W

Did You Know? This iconic landscape has been featured in many popular movies, including *Forrest Gump.*

Rainbow Bridge National Monument

Rainbow Bridge National Monument, one of the world's largest known natural bridges, sees an average of 200,000 to 300,000 visitors per year. Visitors are asked to respect the religious significance of the monument to neighboring tribes and consider viewing the Rainbow Bridge from the viewing area rather than walking up to it. There are two Navajo Mountain trails leading to Rainbow Bridge, which each take at least 2 days total, and continue through canyon country. Both the North Trail and South Trail are over 17 miles and not suitable for a casual hiker. The other way is by boating over Lake Powell. You can take a private vessel or travel on a tour boat. This trail viewing area is approximately 1 mile.

Best Time to Visit: The best time to visit Rainbow Bridge National Monument is in the spring or fall.

Pass/Permit/Fees: There is no fee to visit Rainbow Bridge Monument. The permits required for the Navajo Mountain Trail from Navajo Nation Parks & Recreation are $12 per person per day.

Closest City or Town: Mexican Hat, Utah

Physical Address:
Escalante Interagency Visitor Center
755 W. Main Street
Escalante, UT 84726

GPS Coordinates: 37.0683° N, 111.2433° W

Did You Know? Rainbow Bridge spans 275 feet and has a height of 290 feet.

Homestead Crater

There is a hidden underground cave about an hour outside of Salt Lake City. The Homestead Crater is a geothermal hot spring located inside a 55-foot dome of limestone. The cave is beehive shaped with a hole at the top that welcomes sunlight and fresh air. The inside is heated by the springs, and the water is consistently 90–96°F. The spring is 65 feet deep and 400 feet wide at the base. Its warm temperatures make it a fitting spot for traditional hot-spring soaks, scuba diving, snorkeling, and exploring the crater. You can even paddleboard through the hot spring. There are paddleboard yoga classes offered too.

Best Time to Visit: Visit at any time of the year!

Pass/Permit/Fees: Fees to visit the Homestead Crater vary based on day and soaking time. Monday through Thursday: $13 for swim/soak (40 min.), $18 for snorkeling (40 min.), $22 for a scuba dive (1 hour); Friday through Sunday: $16 for swim/soak (40 min.), $21 for snorkeling (40 min.), $27 for a scuba dive (1 hour).

Closest City or Town: Midway, Utah

Physical Address:
Heber Valley Visitors Center
475 N. Main Street
Heber City, UT 84032

GPS Coordinates: 40.5239° N, 111.4850° W

Did You Know? This crater is the only warm scuba diving destination in the continental U.S.

Ice Castles

This award-winning winter attraction is located in five cities across North America. The Ice Castles are constructed using hundreds of thousands of icicles that are placed by professional ice artists to create incredible ice sculptures, tunnels, fountains, slides, and more. The addition of LED lights embedded within the ice structures turns these majestic creations into awe-inspiring works of art. The attraction opened in 2011 and, because the ice eventually melts, each year's installation is new and different. Ice Castles opens in January and generally closes in early March, but this is dependent upon the weather.

Best Time to Visit: The best time to visit Ice Castles is between January and late March (weather depending).

Pass/Permit/Fees: General admission to Ice Castles is $15 per person on weekdays for visitors ages 12 and up and $11 for visitors ages 4 to 11. On weekends, the price is $22 for adults and $15 for children.

Closest City or Town: Midway, Utah

Physical Address:
2002 Olympic Drive
Midway, UT 84049

GPS Coordinates: 40.48157° N, 111.50067° W

Did You Know? Ice Castles founder Brent Christensen initially built an ice cave in his yard to get his children out of the house during winter.

Memorial Hill

Memorial Hill is a site that is dedicated to Wasatch County citizens who have served in any U.S. military conflict. Once owned by "Uncle" Jesse Hughes McCarrell, the land was purchased by the county for the purpose of providing a memorial to war veterans. Memorial pillars were installed that included brass plaques with the names of veterans engraved on them. Unfortunately, sometime after this initial installation, which was completed in 1927, vandals stole the brass plaques. In 1990, there was a successful effort to collect the names of all Wasatch County veterans to revive the memorial. Today, Memorial Hill displays the names of Wasatch County citizens who have collectively served in 12 wars and conflicts dating back to the War of 1812.

Best Time to Visit: The best time to visit Memorial Hill is in the spring, summer, or fall in the daytime.

Pass/Permit/Fees: There is no fee to visit Memorial Hill.

Closest City or Town: Midway, Utah

Physical Address:
38-40 River Road
Midway, UT, 84049

GPS Coordinates:
40.51759° N, 111.46183° W

Did You Know?
The monument at the top of Memorial Hill is called "The Final Salute."

Rocky Mountain Outfitters

Established in 1997, Rocky Mountain Outfitters is an award-winning adventure-guide company that provides outdoor tours and activities such as horseback riding through the Heber Valley, snowmobiling through the Wasatch Mountains, and fly fishing in the Provo River to Utah visitors. Not only will you get to see the gorgeous Utah landscape, but you'll also get to hear the stories and legends of the area from knowledgeable guides. Special event activities include carriage rides at Jordanelle State Park and horse-drawn sleigh rides to the ice castles.

Best Time to Visit: While Rocky Mountain Outfitters is open all year, not all adventure packages are offered year round. Check the website for package availability.

Pass/Permit/Fees: The fee to visit Rocky Mountain Outfitters depends on the activity or tour you choose. Check the website for pricing details.

Closest City or Town: Midway, Utah

Physical Address:
633 W. Soldier Hollow Lane
Midway, UT 84049

GPS Coordinates: 40.48286° N, 111.48675° W

Did You Know? Rocky Mountain Outfitters is the only company to have a fly shop on the Provo River, a body of water that contains more than 3,000 fish per mile.

Soldier Hollow Nordic Center

Created for the 2002 Winter Olympics, the 21,592-acre Soldier Hollow Nordic Center provides opportunities for cross-country skiing, snowshoeing, tubing, and the biathlon. Visitors can also take a horse-drawn sleigh ride through the mountains from the center. In the summer, it is a venue for mountain biking and golfing, along with special events like the Wasatch Mountain Music Festival and the Soldier Hollow Classic Sheepdog Championship and Festival. The facility was built in 1999 and hosted its first major event, the U.S. Cross Country Skiing Championships, in January 2000. During the 2002 Olympics, Soldier Hollow Nordic Center hosted the Nordic combined, biathlon, and cross-country skiing events. It also hosted the biathlon and cross-country skiing events for the 2002 Winter Paralympics.

Best Time to Visit: The best time to visit the Soldier Hollow Nordic Center is during the winter, even though there are activities available year-round.

Pass/Permit/Fees: The fee to visit the Soldier Hollow Nordic Center depends on your choice of activity.

Closest City or Town: Midway, Utah

Physical Address:
2002 Soldier Hollow Lane
Midway, UT 84049

GPS Coordinates: 40.48155° N, 111.50098° W

Did You Know? The Soldier Hollow Nordic Center is named for its location at the mouth of Soldier Hollow.

Wasatch Mountain State Park

A 23,000-acre preserve located in the Wasatch Mountains, this state park offers year-round recreation, including hiking, mountain biking, camping, horseback riding, golfing, off roading, and more.

In 2002, Wasatch Mountain State Park was the site of several Olympic events, including cross-country skiing and the biathlon. These facilities remain open to the public and have expanded to offer activities like in-line skating and tubing. There are also two historic sites in the park: the Historic Tate Barn and Huber Grove. Tate Barn is a symbol of the Heber Valley, and Huber Grove features the Huber Farmhouse and Creamery. The park was established in 1968 and is Utah's most-developed state park.

Best Time to Visit: The best time to visit Wasatch Mountain State Park depends on the activity you want to try. It is open year round.

Pass/Permit/Fees: There is a $10 fee per vehicle to visit.

Closest City or Town: Midway, Utah

Physical Address:
1281 Warm Springs Road
Midway, UT 84049

GPS Coordinates: 40.53293° N, 111.49018° W

Did You Know? Huber Gove, located in Wasatch Mountain State Park, is home to a 100-year-old apple orchard.

Arches National Park

Arches National Park has the world's largest concentration of natural sandstone arches. There is also an astounding variety of other geological formations, such as colossal sandstone fins, soaring pinnacles, massive rocks, and spires. One option to see the park is via the 36-mile round-trip paved scenic drive that leads visitors to several of the major viewpoints.

There is a wide variety of trails, some as short as 20 minutes, and many of them are rated easy. You can even combine parts of the scenic drive with specific trails to customize your own adventure. Many of these trails lead to formations such as Double Arch, Windows Trail, Delicate Arch, and Devils Garden Trail.

Best Time to Visit: The best times to visit Arches National Park are in the spring and fall.

Pass/Permit/Fees: There is an entry fee of $30 per vehicle, $25 per motorcycle, or $15 per individual to visit Arches National Park, all valid for 7 days.

Closest City or Town: Moab, Utah

Physical Address:
Moab Information Center
25 E. Center Street
Moab, UT 84532

GPS Coordinates: 38.7331° N, 109.5925° W

Did You Know? This park is home to more than 2,000 natural sandstone arches.

Balanced Rock

Located right in the middle of Arches National Park, Balanced Rock towers overhead at a height of 128 feet. A large rock balanced on a narrow pedestal of stone, it is one of the most popular sites at the park. It is located near the park's main road, a little over 9 miles from the entrance. There is an easy, short loop trail of about 0.3 miles that takes you around the base of the rock formation. As the forces of nature continue to erode the rock, the large rock will eventually collapse. This is because the large rock that is balancing on the lower rocks is made of harder material that erodes more slowly.

Best Time to Visit: The best time to visit Balanced Rock is in the spring or fall.

Pass/Permit/Fees: There is an entry fee of $30 per vehicle, $25 per motorcycle, or $15 per individual to visit Balanced Rock, all valid for 7 days.

Closest City or Town: Moab, Utah

Physical Address:
Moab Information Center
25 E. Center Street
Moab, UT 84532

GPS Coordinates: 38.7010° N, 109.5645° W

Did You Know? The rock that is balancing on the upper portion of the formation is as large as three school buses and presumed to weigh 3,577 tons.

Bartlett Wash

This mountain-bike trail is an Entrada sandstone ride that features miles of rock waves and an open-riding area that allows cyclists to freely ride outside a trail. Bartlett Wash features one of the largest open slickrock mountain-biking areas in the world, offering hours of fun for mountain bikers of all skill levels. The trail is officially rated as moderate, but the challenge is significantly lower than it is at Slickrock. In fact, it's a good idea to go to Bartlett Wash before trying the more-difficult ride at Slickrock. There are some scary places at Bartlett Wash for those who want to create a more challenging ride, but if you want to get your wheels under you in Moab, there are plenty of easy places to ride as well.

Best Time to Visit: The best time to visit Bartlett Wash is in the spring or fall to avoid the hottest weather.

Pass/Permit/Fees: There is no fee to visit Bartlett Wash.

Closest City or Town: Moab, Utah

Physical Address:
Moab Information Center
25 E. Center Street
Moab, UT 84532

GPS Coordinates: 38.73165° N, 109.72609° W

Did You Know? The sand at Bartlett Wash is finer than that at Slickrock, so in some places, your wheels will sink in and give you a real workout. Be sure to bring a bicycle-repair kit!

Birthing Rock Petroglyphs

This unique location features ancient rock art on a large boulder adorned with petroglyphs on all four sides. Imagery includes a woman giving birth, centipedes, a hunter with a bow, men fighting, and other interesting figures. The Birthing Rock is one of six sites that comprise the Moab Rock Art Motor Tour along with Moonflower Canyon, Golf Course, Potash Road, Wolf Ranch, and Courthouse Wash.

Best Time to Visit: The best times to visit the Birthing Rock Petroglyphs are in the spring and fall.

Pass/Permit/Fees: There is no fee to visit the Birthing Rock Petroglyphs.

Closest City or Town: Moab, Utah

Physical Address:
Moab Information Center
25 E. Center Street
Moab, UT 84532

GPS Coordinates: 38.5219° N, 109.6027° W

Did You Know? While it is difficult to determine the exact age of rock art, these petroglyphs are believed to have been created somewhere between 500 and 1540 CE.

Canyonlands National Park

This dramatic desert landscape was carved by the Colorado River. The park is divided into four regions, and most people focus on one area per visit. There is no bridge or road that connects the districts in the park. Island in the Sky is the most accessible, boasting a scenic drive featuring views of buttes, canyons, and numerous hikes. Towering rock pinnacles compose the Needles district. This area requires a backcountry approach and involves more strenuous hiking and four-wheel drive. The most isolated district is The Maze. Its remoteness is best accessed by experienced hikers due to its challenging backpacking, off-roading, and hiking trails. You can also book a river trip up the Green or Colorado rivers and see the area by boat.

Best Time to Visit: The best times to visit Canyonlands National Park are in the spring and fall.

Pass/Permit/Fees: There is an entry fee of $30 for private vehicles, $25 for motorcycles, or $15 for pedestrians/bicycles to visit Canyonlands National Park.

Closest City or Town: Moab, Utah

Physical Address:
2282 Resource Boulevard
Moab, UT 84532

GPS Coordinates: 38.2136° N, 109.9025° W

Did You Know? This park covers a total area of 337,598 acres.

Chesler Park Loop/Joint Trail

A 10.4-mile, 6-hour hike, the Chesler Park Loop/Joint Trail is a journey that will make you believe you could be on another planet. It's located in the Needles District of Canyonlands National Park and takes visitors through oddly shaped canyons, rock formations that look like they're melting, and narrow canyon sections that are just shoulder-width apart. Multi-colored rocks, giant boulders, tower-shaped formations, and even grassy meadows seem to pop up out of nowhere on the trail. Be sure to bring your camera because it's almost guaranteed you've seen nothing like the scenery on this trail. Take note of Elephant Hill, the Needles, Druid Arch, Chesler Park, and the Fins of the Maze District while on the hike.

Best Time to Visit: The best time to hike the Chesler Park Loop/Joint Trail is during the spring, fall, or winter.

Pass/Permit/Fees: There is a $30 fee per vehicle to visit the Canyonlands National Park and hike the Chesler Park Loop/Joint Trail.

Closest City or Town: Moab, Utah

Physical Address:
2282 Resource Boulevard
Moab, UT 84532

GPS Coordinates: 38.11089° N, 109.85415° W

Did You Know? The Joint Trail is a 1.5-mile section of the longer Chesler Park Loop and one of the narrowest parts of the hike.

Colorado River

If you're looking for whitewater-rafting adventures, the Colorado River is where you need to be. Often referred to as "the Mighty Colorado River," the intense whitewater rapids are second to none. This river is responsible for carving some of the most incredible canyons in the world, including the Grand Canyon. In Utah, the Colorado River carved Westwater Canyon, Cataract Canyon, Glen Canyon, and Castle Valley. You can access the Colorado River for recreation in any of those places, as there are numerous rafting companies that give tours on the water. Moab is the starting point for many people looking to ride the Colorado River since it's the gateway to several state parks and canyons.

Best Time to Visit: The best time to visit the Colorado River is between April and October. The river is at its wildest in July and August.

Pass/Permit/Fees: There is no fee to visit the Colorado River, but you may need to pay a fee to enter the canyons or parks it passes through or for a river-rafting tour.

Closest City or Town: Moab, Utah

Physical Address:
Moab Information Center
25 E. Center Street
Moab, UT 84532

GPS Coordinates: 38.60416° N, 109.58610° W

Did You Know? About 27 percent of the water used in Utah is sourced from the Colorado River.

Corona Arch

Corona Arch is a 140-foot-wide natural sandstone arch that curves out from a massive stone mountain. This arch is part of the same rock formation as Pinto Arch and Bowtie Arch, which you will pass along the way.

The Corona Arch Trail is 3 miles roundtrip, making it a short hike to a spectacular view. However, this hike is rated as moderately difficult, and safety cables and ladders are involved.

Best Time to Visit: The best time to visit Corona Arch is in the fall or spring.

Pass/Permit/Fees: There is no fee to visit Corona Arch.

Closest City or Town: Moab, Utah

Physical Address:
Moab Information Center
25 E. Center Street
Moab, UT 84532

GPS Coordinates: 38.5799° N, 109.6201° W

Did You Know? Corona Arch is also known as the "Little Rainbow Bridge" due to its resemblance to the famous Rainbow Bridge.

Dead Horse Point State Park

This park features incredible overlooks of the Colorado River and Canyonlands National Park. The scenic vistas of this area are some of the most photographed in the world. The overlook is 2,000 feet above the Colorado River. With 8 miles of connected hiking trails that lead to eight different overlooks, there is a lot of canyon country to see. The Intrepid Trail System is an eight-segment mountain-biking trail of over 16 miles to ride and enjoy spectacular views. Rated as easy through moderate, many of the bike trails are family friendly. The Dead Horse Point State Park is designated as an International Dark Sky Park, and camping is available nearby.

Best Time to Visit: Visit during the spring or fall.

Pass/Permit/Fees: There is an entry fee of $20 per vehicle, $10 per motorcycle, or $4 per pedestrian/cyclist to visit Dead Horse Point State Park, all valid for 2 consecutive days.

Closest City or Town: Moab, Utah

Physical Address:
Moab Information Center
25 E. Center Street
Moab, UT 84532

GPS Coordinates: 38.4748° N, 109.7406° W

Did You Know? Legend says the park was named Dead Horse because it was used as a natural corral by cowboys long ago, and the horses would sadly often die of exposure.

Delicate Arch

Delicate Arch is a massive, red-hued, standalone arch in the eastern part of Arches National Park. With an opening that is 46 feet high and 32 feet wide, it is the largest freestanding arch in the park. The trail to the arch is 3 miles round trip at a steady incline up to 480 feet. It is rated as moderate. There is also a more easily accessible viewpoint on a lower trail called the Lower Delicate Arch Viewpoint. The less visually obstructed Upper Viewpoint is a short distance away.

Best Time to Visit: The best time to visit Delicate Arch is in the spring or fall.

Pass/Permit/Fees: There is an entry fee of $30 per vehicle, $25 per motorcycle, or $15 per individual to visit Delicate Arch, all valid for 7 days.

Closest City or Town: Moab, Utah

Physical Address:
Moab Information Center
25 E. Center Street
Moab, UT 84532

GPS Coordinates: 38.7436° N, 109.4993° W

Did You Know? Delicate Arch has become a widely recognized symbol of the state of Utah and is featured on state license plates.

Devils Garden Trails

Devils Garden is on the north side of Arches National Park. In this portion of the area, you'll find arches, spires, narrow rock walls, and breathtaking views. The crown jewel, Landscape Arch, is the longest natural rock span in the world. It sits to the north in Devils Garden, and its opening is an awe-inspiring 306 feet. The Landscape Arch trail is an easy segment, but the trails get more difficult beyond the arch. The Double O Arch trail is strenuous, and the alternate route called Primitive Trail is the most difficult segment of the trail system. The entire loop is 7.8 miles. Along with the spectacular views of the area, Devils Garden also offers activities for every skill level, including camping, backpacking, hiking, and stargazing.

Best Time to Visit: The best time to visit Devils Garden Trails is in the spring or fall.

Pass/Permit/Fees: There is an entry fee of $30 per vehicle, $25 per motorcycle, or $15 per individual to visit the Devils Garden Trails, all valid for 7 days.

Closest City or Town: Moab, Utah

Physical Address:
Moab Information Center
25 E. Center Street
Moab, UT 84532

GPS Coordinates: 38.7829° N, 109.5949° W

Did You Know? There is a 150-foot monolith named Dark Angel in Devils Garden.

Double Arch

This double arch is the tallest and second-longest arch in Arches National Park. It is within the Windows area and a short walk from the Windows Arches. The larger opening is 148 feet wide and 104 feet high. It's a short half-mile and mostly flat hike along the Double Arch Trail to get to the formation. The arch is unique because it was formed differently from others in the park. It is known as a "pothole arch" because the water erosion occurred from above the arch rather than the side.

Best Time to Visit: The best time to visit Double Arch is in the spring or fall.

Pass/Permit/Fees: There is an entry fee of $30 per vehicle, $25 per motorcycle, or $15 per individual, all valid for 7 days.

Closest City or Town: Moab, Utah

Physical Address:
Moab Information Center
25 E. Center Street
Moab, UT 84532

GPS Coordinates: 38.6916° N, 109.5403° W

Did You Know? Double Arch was featured in a scene from the movie *Indiana Jones and the Last Crusade.*

Faux Waterfalls

It is just a short hike to get to this beautiful desert waterfall. There's even a swimming hole at the base, so bring your swimsuit! The waterfall is very close to Ken's Lake. There are cottonwoods and desert flowers with the scenic cliff as a backdrop. The drive to the trailhead is somewhat rocky, and a four-wheel-drive vehicle is recommended.

Best Time to Visit: The best time to visit Faux Waterfalls is in the summer for swimming, but it's excellent to visit all year long.

Pass/Permit/Fees: There is no fee to visit Faux Waterfalls.

Closest City or Town: Moab, Utah

Physical Address:
Moab Information Center
25 E. Center Street
Moab, UT 84532

GPS Coordinates: 38.4811° N, 109.4117° W

Did You Know? The waterfall is called a faux waterfall because it's a man-made feature using a diversion tunnel from Mill Creek.

Fiery Furnace

Within Arches National Park, the Fiery Furnace is found. This natural sandstone feature is a meandering labyrinth of sandstone fins that often requires the assistance of a ranger to get through since navigation equipment like GPS doesn't work well in the narrow canyons. The landscaping is confusing, so there are only two ways visitors can legally enter the Fiery Furnace. Visitors can join a ranger-led tour at the Visitor Center to avoid getting lost in the extensive passages. It is not recommended that first time visitors obtain a permit from the Visitor Center and go on their own without a guide.

Best Time to Visit: The best time to visit the Fiery Furnace is between March and October when the ranger-led tours are offered.

Pass/Permit/Fees: There is a $30 fee per vehicle to visit Arches National Park and hike through the Fiery Furnace. There is also a $16 fee per person to join a ranger-led tour.

Closest City or Town: Moab, Utah

Physical Address:
Moab Information Center
25 E. Center Street
Moab, UT 84532

GPS Coordinates: 38.74428° N, 109.56167° W

Did You Know? Tickets for ranger-led tours through the Fiery Furnace sell out quickly, so the earlier you purchase your spot, the better.

Ken's Lake

Ken's Lake Campground is part of the Ken's Lake Recreation Area. The entire area includes the lake, the campground, a man-made reservoir, a day-use area equipped with a boat ramp, and trails to hike or explore via horseback. Three miles of trails are within the vicinity of the lake. The trails feature views of the Moab Valley and the La Sal Mountains. The lake is kept stocked with fish, but a Utah fishing license is required if you are over 14 years old. Surrounded by arid desert, Ken's Lake is a perfect place to come and escape the heat. You can swim, fish, and paddle here.

Best Time to Visit: Ken's Lake is excellent to visit any time of the year.

Pass/Permit/Fees: There is a $20 camping fee per site to stay overnight at Ken's Lake. There is no day-use fee.

Closest City or Town: Moab, Utah

Physical Address:
Moab Information Center
25 E. Center Street
Moab, UT 84532

GPS Coordinates: 38.4815° N, 109.4296° W

Did You Know? Ken's Lake is a part of an initiative called the Mills Creek Project that helps provide an irrigation system.

Mesa Arch

Mesa Arch is a popular destination in Canyonlands National Park that features an often-photographed natural sandstone arch. It is located on the edge of a cliff, which provides spectacular views of rock spires, canyons, and the La Sal Mountains. There is a 0.8-mile hike to Mesa Arch that is rated as moderate, but it is well marked, and you'll even see signs that point out plants that are common in the Canyonlands along with their traditional uses. Photographers flock to Mesa Arch to get the once-in-a-lifetime shot of the sun rising beyond the arch, so be prepared for crowds in the early mornings. If you don't get a sunrise shot, though, don't give up! There are plenty of other opportunities to get stunning photographs of the arch with the changing light throughout the day.

Best Time to Visit: Visit is in spring, summer, or fall before dawn. To avoid crowds, visit later in the day.

Pass/Permit/Fees: There is a $30 fee per vehicle, per week to visit Canyonlands National Park.

Closest City or Town: Moab, Utah

Physical Address:
2282 Resource Boulevard
Moab, UT 84532

GPS Coordinates: 38.38884° N, 109.86377° W

Did You Know? Mesa Arch is known as a pothole arch because it was formed when surface water pooled on the sandstone behind where the arch would form, slowly eroding the rock.

Needles Overlook

At 1,600 feet above the Needles District of Canyonlands National Park, the Needles Overlook provides a 360-degree view of the sandstone formations that surround the park. The overlook is actually located outside Canyonlands National Park, about 22 miles off of Highway 191. If you're traveling between Moab and Monticello, the Needles Overlook is a must-stop destination. It's especially gorgeous at sunset and is a popular area for professional (and amateur) photographers. Unlike most overlooks, the Needles Overlook is not just a single platform with a view over a canyon. Instead, it is a ledge that allows you to walk around the entire cliff to get a full experience of the park and canyons. Most people spend at least an hour walking around the edge and taking in the impressive view.

Best Time to Visit: The best time to visit Needles Overlook is at sunset any time of the year.

Pass/Permit/Fees: There is no fee to visit.

Closest City or Town: Moab, Utah

Physical Address:
Moab Information Center
25 E. Center Street
Moab, UT 84532

GPS Coordinates: 38.26076° N, 109.69596° W

Did You Know? From Needles Overlook, visitors can see the 11,000-foot Henry Mountains over 60 miles away.

Sand Flats Recreation Area

The Sand Flats Recreation Area is home to the Slickrock mountain-biking trail, but it also boasts numerous other outdoor activities that draw more than 200,000 people to the area each year. At 9,000 acres in size, there is plenty of space for everyone to enjoy camping, hiking, 4x4 driving, sightseeing. In the Sand Flats Recreation Area, there are trails for mountain bikers of all skill levels, including scenic rides for beginners and highly technical rides for those looking for a challenge. Moab is revered as the best mountain-biking location in the world, so whether you've just taken up the sport or you've been doing it your whole life, you simply must try your hand at these trails.

Best Time to Visit: The best time to visit is during the spring or fall to avoid the hottest weather.

Pass/Permit/Fees: There is a $5 fee per person for a day pass or a $10 fee per person for a 7-day pass to visit.

Closest City or Town: Moab, Uta

Physical Address:
Moab Information Center
25 E. Center Street
Moab, UT 84532

GPS Coordinates: 38.57727° N, 109.51874° W

Did You Know? There is no water on the trails in the Sand Flats Recreation Area, so you'll need to bring your own. Experts recommend you bring at least a gallon of water per person per day.

Shafer Trail Road

Located in the Sky District of Canyonlands National Park, the Shafer Trail Road is a popular attraction that descends 1,500 feet through a massive sandstone canyon. It is a challenging, unpaved road that provides a thrill for adventure seekers who want to get off the main roads and into the backcountry. The trail has served various purposes over the years, from a route Native Americans took to get supplies to the top of the mesa to a trail used by sheep herders. Today, however, it is solely used as a recreational road and sometimes as the backdrop for Hollywood movies.

Best Time to Visit: The best time to visit Shafer Trail Road is between May and October. It is closed during the winter.

Pass/Permit/Fees: There is no fee to drive Shafer Trail Road, but there is a $30 fee per vehicle to enter Canyonlands National Park. The pass is valid for 7 days.

Closest City or Town: Moab, Utah

Physical Address:
Canyonlands National Park
2282 Resource Boulevard
Moab, UT 84532

GPS Coordinates: 38.44927° N, 109.82175° W

Did You Know? Shafer Trail Road is named for the Shafer family of Mormon pioneers who settled in the area.

Slickrock Trail

A world-famous mountain-biking trail, Slickrock Trail is a 10.6-mile loop that is rated difficult. The variable terrain along the sandstone path makes it even more challenging, and if your bike is not up to it, parts might rattle loose. Sections of the route are extremely steep, and most cyclists end up pushing their bike up some of the slopes. Overall, the trail involves more than 2,500 vertical feet of climbing. The Navajo Sandstone trail developed more than 200 million years ago and with time and erosion has developed into domes and mounds that make for fun—and challenging—mountain biking. There is a practice loop for new riders.

Best Time to Visit: Ride Slickrock Trail is spring or fall because it can get extremely hot in the summer.

Pass/Permit/Fees: There is a $2 daily fee per person to ride the Slickrock Trail. Riders can also pay $5 for a 7-day pass.

Closest City or Town: Moab, Utah

Physical Address:
Moab Information Center
25 E. Center Street
Moab, UT 84532

GPS Coordinates: 38.58247° N, 109.51936° W

Did You Know? The Slickrock Trail was originally constructed in 1969 for use by Honda Trail 90s (motorbikes) but was converted to accommodate mountain bikes when motorbikes were outlawed.

Thelma & Louise Point

Located in Moab, Thelma & Louise Point is the actual cliff where the main characters of the movie *Thelma & Louise* drove their car off the road as they ran from the law. The canyon where this point is situated, which is in Canyonlands National Park, is often referred to as the "Grand Canyon stunt double" because movies cannot be filmed at the actual Grand Canyon, and this area closely resembles the geography. There is no information that indicates this is the cliff where the movie was filmed, but when comparing the actual landscape with the scene, there's no doubt about it being the same cliff. Thelma & Louise Point is only accessible by driving the Shafer Trail, which is closed in the winter.

Best Time to Visit: The best time to visit Thelma & Louise Point is during the spring, summer, or fall.

Pass/Permit/Fees: There is a $30 fee per vehicle to visit Thelma & Louise Point.

Closest City or Town: Moab, Utah

Physical Address:
Canyonland National Park
2282 Resource Boulevard
Moab, UT 84532

GPS Coordinates: 38.45256° N, 109.73483° W

Did You Know? Along the route to Thelma & Louise Point, there are other spots that were also filming locations you might recognize if you're a fan of the movie.

Windows Trail

Windows Trail is a leisurely trail in Arches National Park that can take you to other parts of the area. This easy trail is about a mile long and visits three impressive arches along the way. The main attraction is the two arches standing side by side, separated by some distance. They're known as the North Window and South Window. These two arches are cut from the same sandstone fin, with a gigantic fin remnant of over 100 feet wide between them. The Turret Arch is southwest of these "windows." It sits within a tower-like rock formation. The entire area is full of captivating stone formations.

Best Time to Visit: The best time to visit Windows Trail is in the spring or fall.

Pass/Permit/Fees: There is an entry fee of $30 per vehicle, $25 per motorcycle, or $15 per individual to visit Windows Trail, all valid for 7 days.

Closest City or Town: Moab, Utah

Physical Address:
Moab Information Center
25 E. Center Street
Moab, UT 84532

GPS Coordinates: 38.6872° N, 109.5367° W

Did You Know? The North and South Window Arches are often referred to as "The Spectacles" because they look like a pair of glasses when viewed from a distance.

Newspaper Rock

Newspaper Rock is one of the most famous rock-art sites in the Western United States. For more than 2,000 years, Native Americans have been drawing and engraving their art on this rock, which tells their stories of hunting, crop cycles, and mythology. It represents the largest collection of petroglyphs in the U.S. and features drawings from Ute, Anasazi, and Fremont tribes. More than 650 designs of human figures, animals, symbols, and presumably religious markings have been drawn on and carved into the rock. They were created by chipping away the black desert covering to the lighter rock below. The 200-square-foot rock belongs to Indian Creek Canyon. Newspaper Rock became a State Historical Monument in 1961 and was added to the National Register of Historic Places in 1976.

Best Time to Visit: The best time to visit Newspaper Rock is during the daytime in the spring, summer, or fall.

Pass/Permit/Fees: There is no fee to visit.

Closest City or Town: Monticello, Utah

Physical Address:
Monticello Welcome Center
216 S. Main Street
Monticello, UT 84535

GPS Coordinates: 37.98909° N, 109.51805° W

Did You Know? In the Navajo language, Newspaper Rock is called *Tse' Hone'*, which means "rock that tells a story."

Mystic Hot Springs

Formerly known as Monroe Hot Springs, this location boasts that it's "the best hippie hot springs in the West." The pure mineral water provides a spectacular soaking experience and is naturally heated by the Earth. The spring water emerges from the ground at 168°F and cools to around 100°F as it flows to the smaller pools.

With two concrete pools and six vintage cast-iron tubs to choose from in the secluded area, you can enjoy a breathtaking Utah sunset or the Milky Way after dark. There is also an acoustic concert venue to enjoy live music while you relax in the warm water.

Best Time to Visit: The best time to visit Mystic Hot Springs is during the early spring or fall to avoid crowds.

Pass/Permit/Fees: There is a $25 soaking pass fee per person to visit Mystic Hot Springs. Reservations are required for a 2-hour time slot.

Closest City or Town: Monroe, Utah

Physical Address:
475 E. 100 North
Monroe, UT 84754

GPS Coordinates: 38.6343° N, 112.1090° W

Did You Know? Water from the hot springs carries calcium carbonate, magnesium, and iron.

25th Street Historic District

The 25th Street Historic District is best known as the location of Union Station, a train station that was built during the construction of the Transcontinental Railroad in 1869. It was located a short distance from the main train depot where the rail lines converged. This major hub gave rise to restaurants and hotels to provide travelers with eating and lodging options when they were waiting for their trains to arrive. Eventually, a third rail line, this one for the Utah Northern Railroad, also converged at Union Station. Unfortunately, the original station was destroyed by fire in 1923. 25th Street became a center of activity in the 20th century, and with the addition of art galleries, a farmers market, and numerous community events, the district remains a popular attraction today.

Best Time to Visit: The best time to visit the 25th Street Historic District is between June and August.

Pass/Permit/Fees: There is no fee to visit.

Closest City or Town: Ogden, Utah

Physical Address:
Visit Ogden
2411 Kiesel Avenue, Ste 401
Ogden, UT 84401

GPS Coordinates: 41.22330° N, 111.97208° W

Did You Know? The television series *Everwood* (2002) and the movie *Drive Me Crazy* (1999) were partially filmed in the 25th Street Historic District.

Dinosaur Park and Museum

With more than 1,254 dinosaur sculptures across 8 acres, Dinosaur Park and Museum will thrill anyone who is fascinated by these incredible prehistoric animals. Each sculpture is full sized based on actual fossils and skeletons, and they contain robotic parts that allow them to move realistically. A cutting-edge sound system allows visitors to hear what it might have sounded like to witness these magnificent creatures in person. The 16,000-square-foot indoor museum features various exhibits, a paleontology laboratory, and a lecture hall.

Best Time to Visit: The Dinosaur Park and Museum is open Wednesday through Saturday from 10:00 a.m. to 5:00 p.m. in the winter, Monday through Saturday from 10:00 a.m. to 5:00 p.m. in the spring, and Monday through Saturday from 10:00 a.m. to 7:00 p.m. in the summer.

Pass/Permit/Fees: Admission to the Dinosaur Park and Museum is $7 for adults, $5 for children ages 2 to 12, and $6 for students ages 13 to 17 or seniors ages 62 and up.

Closest City or Town: Ogden, Utah

Physical Address:
1544 E. Park Boulevard
Ogden, UT 84401

GPS Coordinates: 41.23857° N, 111.93777° W

Did You Know? The Education Center at the Dinosaur Park and Museum offers a hands-on Stegosaurus dig.

Great Salt Lake & Antelope Island

The largest saltwater lake in the Western Hemisphere, the Great Salt Lake is also the largest lake between the Pacific Ocean and the Great Lakes. At 12 percent salinity, it is saltier than the ocean, so it's easy to float in the water. Considered to be one of the best ways to enjoy the lake, Antelope Island State Park offers an ideal place to swim and sunbathe along the white-sand beaches. You can also kayak and sail. There are full-service marinas available at Antelope Island and the southern shore of the lake. Antelope Island and Stansbury Island also feature excellent mountain-biking trails.

Best Time to Visit: The best time to visit the Great Salt Lake and Antelope Island is in the fall.

Pass/Permit/Fees: There is an entry fee of $15 per vehicle or $3 per bicycle/motorcycle/pedestrian to visit Great Salt Lake and Antelope Island.

Closest City or Town: Ogden, Utah

Physical Address:
Antelope Island State Park
4528 W. 1700 South
Syracuse, UT 84075

GPS Coordinates: 41.1158° N, 112.4768° W

Did You Know? The average depth of Great Salt Lake is 20 feet, and the maximum depth is 33 feet.

Hill Aerospace Museum

Founded in 1981, the Hill Aerospace Museum is part of the United States Air Force Heritage Program and displays more than 70 aircraft in its two indoor galleries and one outdoor air park. Visitors will also discover thousands of aviation-related artifacts that tell the story of aviation history in the United States. Its collection of aircraft includes attack aircraft, bombers, cargo planes, fighters, helicopters, surveillance, and trainers. There are also examples of early aircraft, gliders, and light aircraft. It is currently located on the northwest corner of Hill Air Force Base and offers unique learning experiences to inspire and ignite the passion of flight in visitors.

Best Time to Visit: The Hill Aerospace Museum is open Tuesday through Saturday from 9:00 a.m. to 4:00 p.m.

Pass/Permit/Fees: There is no fee to visit the Hill Aerospace Museum, but donations are appreciated.

Closest City or Town: Ogden, Utah

Physical Address:
7961 Cottonwood Street, Building 1955
Hill Air Force Base, UT 84056

GPS Coordinates: 41.16208° N, 112.01961° W

Did You Know? Approximately 350,000 guests visit the Hill Aerospace Museum each year, and it hosted its 5 millionth visitor in 2019.

Waterfall Canyon

Located just above the city of Ogden, Waterfall Canyon is home to a 300-foot waterfall cascade found at the upper end of the canyon.

The Waterfall Canyon trail is 2.4 miles in and out and accessible all year round. The steep, rocky hike is worth it for the view of the waterfall and the valley. There are several trails to explore that are clearly marked, but be aware that these trails are surrounded by private property.

The main trail begins at a large parking lot next to a residential tower. There are several more that branch out from this area, so ensure you follow the Bonneville Shoreline Trail (BST).

Best Time to Visit: The best times to visit Waterfall Canyon are early spring or late fall to avoid crowds.

Pass/Permit/Fees: There is no fee to visit Waterfall Canyon.

Closest City or Town: Ogden, Utah

Physical Address:
29th Street Trailhead
Waterfall Canyon Trail
Ogden, UT 84403

GPS Coordinates: 41.21150° N, 111.93193° W

Did You Know? Malan Falls is the unofficial name of the waterfall, named for the family that used to own the land in the area.

Zion Ponderosa Ranch Resort

The Zion Ponderosa Ranch Resort offers ideal accommodations for nature lovers. It is a full-service, 4,000-acre ranch resort that offers an authentic Western experience with horseback riding and Western-style meals. There are many on-resort activities available, including canyoneering, Jeep tours, guided hiking, rock climbing (on a climbing wall), miniature golf, a trampoline bungee, a zip line, paintball, a shotgun range, a recreation barn, tennis, horseshoes, volleyball, a two-tiered swimming pool, and two hot tubs. Guests can choose glamping tents, furnished Conestoga Wagons, cowboy cabins, vacation homes, or cabin suites for their accommodations, all of which offer modern amenities such as electricity, heat, and Wi-Fi. There's no need to rough it when you visit Zion National Park.

Best Time to Visit: The best time to visit Zion Ponderosa Ranch Resort is during the spring, summer, or fall.

Pass/Permit/Fees: Fees vary. Check the website for detailed pricing information.

Closest City or Town: Orderville, Utah

Physical Address:
Twin Knolls Road
Orderville, UT 84758

GPS Coordinates: 37.27066° N, 112.87586° W

Did You Know? Zion Ponderosa Ranch is 6,500 feet above sea level.

Red Canyon

Called the "most photographed place in Utah," this canyon in the Dixie National Forest is exceptionally scenic with Ponderosa pines set against a background of red sandstone and spires. There are views of hoodoo formations, red cliffs, and pink soil too. The trails are extensive and well maintained. Birdseye Trail is a 0.8-mile hike featuring close-up views of the red-rock formations. Losee Canyon Trail is 3 miles and provides a more rugged trek. Casto Canyon trail allows for off-highway vehicle usage, but you should check with the visitor center about off-road trail use. There is the Red Canyon Travel Kiosk, located just east of the visitor center, where five different trails can be accessed. You will definitely want a map!

Best Time to Visit: The best time to visit Red Canyon is between May and September.

Pass/Permit/Fees: There is no fee to visit Red Canyon.

Closest City or Town: Panguitch, Utah

Physical Address:
Red Canyon Visitor Center
5375 UT-12
Panguitch, UT 84759

GPS Coordinates: 37.7458° N, 112.3380° W

Did You Know? The landscape of Red Canyon is very similar to the famous Bryce Canyon, just on a smaller scale.

Egyptian Theatre

A centerpiece of Park City culture, the Egyptian Theatre presents live performances in a historical setting. The Egyptian Theatre was built between 1922 and 1926 on the site of the former Dewey Theatre, which enjoyed full audiences between 1899 and 1916 until its roof collapsed under a record-setting snow load. The new theater's architecture and décor were inspired by the discovery of King Tut's tomb in November 1922, and the interior is adorned with scarabs, hieroglyphics, and lotus-leaf motifs. Currently, the Egyptian Theatre hosts comedy shows, musical acts, special events, and of course, live theatre performances.

Best Time to Visit: The best time to visit the Egyptian Theatre is when there is a show playing that you want to see. Check the website for dates and showtimes.

Pass/Permit/Fees: The fee to visit the Egyptian Theatre depends on show and seat selection. See the website for pricing details.

Closest City or Town: Park City, Utah

Physical Address:
328 Main Street
Park City, UT 84060

GPS Coordinates: 40.64335° N, 111.49520° W

Did You Know? Before it became the Dewey Theatre and the Egyptian Theatre, the site was home to the Park City Opera House and was destroyed by fire in 1898.

Guardsman Pass Scenic Backway

For some of the most incredible mountain views, travel the Guardsman Pass Scenic Backway, a 24.2-mile paved road that takes visitors to the summit of Big Cottonwood Canyon in the Wasatch Mountain Range. It runs from Park City to Brighton or Midway. The drive takes about 1 hour if you don't stop, but you'll definitely want to stop, especially at the summit where the views are breathtaking. There's a little bit of everything along the way, including alpine panoramas, clear lakes, trickling creeks, and rushing rivers. Be aware that the road is not plowed in the winter, so even though the views might be spectacular after a recent snowfall, you won't be able to access the road between at least November and April.

Best Time to Visit: The best time to drive the Guardsman Pass Scenic Backway is during the fall when the leaves on the trees are changing color.

Pass/Permit/Fees: There is no fee to drive the Guardsman Pass Scenic Backway.

Closest City or Town: Park City, Utah

Physical Address:
Park City Visitors Center
1794 Olympic Parkway
Park City, UT 84098

GPS Coordinates: 40.60757° N, 111.55512° W

Did You Know? At its peak, the Guardsman Pass Scenic Byway is approximately 9,700 feet above sea level

Historic Main Street

Park City was once the base camp of a silver mine, but today, its Historic Main Street is one of the most popular mountain towns in Utah and possibly in the western U.S. It is packed with luxury boutiques, art galleries, eclectic independent restaurants of every type, and plenty of bars, breweries, and distilleries for that after-skiing drink. Restaurants like Riverhorse on Main, Grappa Italian Café, Handle, High West Saloon, and Yuki Yama Sushi draw visitors from all over the state, even those who aren't die-hard skiers. You're also sure to find a treasure or two in shops like Alpaca International, Gallery Mar, McMillen Fine Art Photography, Olive & Tweed, and more. If you visit during the summer, be sure to attend Park Silly, an incredible farmers market that's held every Sunday from June through September.

Best Time to Visit: The best time to visit Historic Main Street in Park City is during the ski season.

Pass/Permit/Fees: There is no fee to visit.

Closest City or Town: Park City, Utah

Physical Address:
Main Street Visitor Center
544 Main Street
Park City, UT 84098

GPS Coordinates: 40.64479° N, 111.49626° W

Did You Know? Utah's first legal brewery and distillery—the Wasatch Brewery and High West Distillery—are both located on Main Street in Park City.

Jordanelle Reservoir

Filled by the Provo River, Jordanelle Reservoir provides culinary water to residents in Wasatch and Salt Lake counties. The Jordanelle Swim Beach provides day-use water and beach activities like swimming; nonmotorized boating (canoeing, kayaking, paddleboarding); picnicking; sunbathing; and beach sports like volleyball and Frisbee. The beach sand is coarse, like most of the beaches in the area, but it's large enough to handle the crowds that seek relief from the summer heat. Boats and paddleboards can be rented at the beach, and there's a geocache adventure called "A Journey Through the Solar System" that's a fun activity for kids.

Best Time to Visit: The best time to visit the Jordanelle Reservoir is during the summer.

Pass/Permit/Fees: There is a $20 fee per vehicle to visit the Jordanelle Reservoir.

Closest City or Town: Park City, Utah

Physical Address:
475 N. Main Street
Heber City, UT 84032

GPS Coordinates: 40.62803° N, 111.40927° W

Did You Know? At the top of the Jordanelle Reservoir is the Aqua x Zone, an inflatable water-sports park that is open to swimmers ages 6 and up.

Kimball Art Center

Located in Park City, the Kimball Art Center is dedicated to providing international art exhibitions and unique educational opportunities for the residents and visitors of Park City, Wasatch County, and Summit County. The center was founded in 1976 by Bill Kimball and is one of the oldest cultural nonprofit organizations in the region. To achieve its mission to "inspire and connect through art," the center provides free art-education programs to Utah schools and free art exhibitions in its galleries. The Kimball Art Center is currently located in a temporary building but will move to its permanent home in the coming years.

Best Time to Visit: The Kimball Art Center is open Tuesday through Thursday from 10:00 a.m. to 6:00 p.m., Friday from 10:00 a.m. to 8:00 p.m., and weekends from 10:00 a.m. to 5:00 p.m.

Pass/Permit/Fees: There is no fee to visit the Kimball Art Center.

Closest City or Town: Park City, Utah

Physical Address:
1251 Kearns Boulevard
Park City, UT 84060
(Temporary location)

GPS Coordinates: 40.66164° N, 111.50368° W

Did You Know? From its inception in 1976 until 2016, the Kimball Art Center was housed at the Ely Garage on the corner of Heber and Park avenues.

Park City Museum

The Park City Museum is located on Historic Main Street, one of numerous attractions along this famous mining-town street. It's an award-winning museum that tells the fascinating story of how the town sprung up after prospectors discovered silver in the area in 1868 and reinvented itself as a skiing mecca after silver prices dropped in the early 1950s. The city lost nearly a third of its population during this time, so city leaders had to refocus efforts on tourism to keep the town alive.

Best Time to Visit: The Park City Museum is open daily from 10:00 a.m. to 5:00 p.m.

Pass/Permit/Fees: Admission is $15 for adults and $11 for military members. Seniors ages 65 and up, children ages 7 to 17, and students cost $5. Children ages 6 and under are free.

Closest City or Town: Park City, Utah

Physical Address:
528 Main Street
Park City, UT 84060

GPS Coordinates: 40.64527° N, 111.49624° W

Did You Know? During the 10 days of the 2002 Winter Olympics, more than 25,000 people visited the Park City Museum. It usually sees about 130,000 visitors each year.

Utah Olympic Park

Utah Olympic Park was constructed specifically for the 2002 Olympic Winter Games. It houses a sliding track, six Nordic ski jumps, and a 2002 Winter Games Museum, among other exciting activities. Visitors from all over the world come to Utah Olympic Park to participate in activities like the Winter Bobsled Experience, the UOP Junior Skeleton Program, ice skating on the "fastest ice on Earth," Cosmic Curling, winter tubing, and more. Groups can also rent out the facility for meetings, team-building retreats, and other large-scale events.

Best Time to Visit: The best time to visit Utah Olympic Park depends on when an activity or event is happening that you want to experience. Check the website for dates and times.

Pass/Permit/Fees: The fee to visit Utah Olympic Park depends on the activity or event you're attending. Public ice skating is $6 per person for adults, $5 for seniors ages 65 and up, and $5 for children ages 12 and under.

Closest City or Town: Park City, Utah

Physical Address:
3419 Olympic Parkway
Park City, UT 84098

GPS Coordinates: 40.71252° N, 111.56189° W

Did You Know? More Olympic world records have been set on the 400-meter Utah Olympic Oval at the Utah Olympic Park than anywhere else in the world.

Alpine Loop Scenic Byway

A side trip available from the Provo Canyon Scenic Byway, the Alpine Loop Scenic Byway is a 20-mile drive through the Wasatch Mountain that features spectacular views of Mount Timpanogos and other towering peaks. The byway follows Utah Highway 92 up through the American Fork Canyon and into the Uinta National Forest. If you have time, take a quick detour to Cascade Springs, a mountain spring that includes a 0.25-mile boardwalk that takes you out over natural, clear pools filled with fish and aquatic plants.

Best Time to Visit: The Alpine Loop Scenic Byway closes from November to late May, so the best time to visit is between June and October.

Pass/Permit/Fees: While there is no fee to drive the Alpine Loop Scenic Byway, there is a $6 fee per vehicle to use the facilities along the route. It is valid for 3 days.

Closest City or Town: Provo, Utah

Physical Address:
Provo/Utah Valley Visitor's Center
220 W. Center Street
Provo, UT 84601

GPS Coordinates: 40.43379° N, 111.63600° W

Did You Know? The Alpine Loop Scenic Byway is also referred to as the "Road to Nowhere" because it really doesn't lead anywhere.

BYU Museum of Paleontology

The BYU Museum of Paleontology was established in 1976 to prepare, exhibit, and house the dinosaur and rock fossils discovered and collected by Dr. James A Jensen and his paleontology teams. These fossils were collected throughout Utah, Montana, Wyoming, and Colorado. The relatively small museum makes the most of its space by creating spectacular exhibits that encourage visitors to engage with the past. There are full triceratops and *Tyrannosaurus rex* skulls on display as well as a complete skeleton of a giant sloth. There's even a viewing window where visitors can watch the museum's paleontologists work on real fossils. There are some fossils placed throughout the museum that visitors can touch and an entire room dedicated to plant and non-dinosaur animal fossils.

Best Time to Visit: The museum is open Monday through Friday from 9:00 a.m. to 5:00 p.m.

Pass/Permit/Fees: There is no fee to visit the museum.

Closest City or Town: Provo, Utah

Physical Address:
1683 N. Canyon Road
Provo, UT 84602

GPS Coordinates: 40.25718° N, 111.65648° W

Did You Know? Until the museum was built, the vast, unprepared fossil collections were stored under the BYU football stadium.

Diamond Fork Hot Springs

The warm, cobalt-blue water of the Diamond Fork Hot Springs is both lovely to see and great for a relaxing soak. Several pools are available for soaking, with the sounds and views of three lovely waterfalls nearby. The forestry and red cliffs provide the perfect backdrop to the area. The trail to the hot springs is a little over 2 miles from the trailhead, with a gradual elevation gain of 700 feet. The first half follows along the left side of Sixth Water Creek, and you will know when you are approaching the hot springs from the smell of the sulfur. If visiting in the winter, you might need to bring snowshoes if the snow isn't packed down on the trail. There is a road closure due to snow in the winter, so the trek is a bit longer.

Best Time to Visit: The best time to visit Diamond Fork Hot Springs is between September and early November to avoid crowds.

Pass/Permit/Fees: There is no fee to visit Diamond Fork Hot Springs.

Closest City or Town: Provo, Utah

Physical Address:
Springville Civic Center
110 S. Main Street
Springville, UT 84663

GPS Coordinates: 40.0845° N, 111.3550° W

Did You Know? Diamond Fork Hot Springs used to be called Fifth Water Hot Springs.

Museum of Peoples and Cultures

Located on the Brigham Young University campus, the Museum of Peoples and Cultures has its roots as a natural history, geological, and archaeological museum from 1879. It was established by James E. Talmage. That institution would eventually evolve into four separate museums of which the Museum of Peoples and Cultures is one. The other three are the Paleontology Museum, the Museum of Art, and the Monte L. Bean Life Science Museum. The Museum of Peoples and Cultures holds the university's archaeological and anthropological collections. When BYU's archaeology department opened in 1946, the subsequent research and field work generated thousands of artifacts that necessitated the formation of a museum.

Best Time to Visit: The Museum of Peoples and Cultures is open Monday through Friday from 9:00 a.m. to 5:00 p.m.

Pass/Permit/Fees: There is no fee to visit.

Closest City or Town: Provo, Utah

Physical Address:
2201 N. Canyon Road
Provo, UT 84604

GPS Coordinates: 40.26383° N, 111.65746° W

Did You Know? It is housed in Allen Hall, a former men's dormitory built in the 1930s.

Provo Beach

Considered Utah's premier center for families, Provo Beach offers 50,000 square feet of fun. Attractions include an indoor FlowRider (a wave machine that produces 30,000 gallons of water each minute and allows for a highly realistic surfing experience), a ropes course, laser tag, miniature croquet, bowling, a carousel, playgrounds, and arcade games. Visitors never have to worry about the weather outside because these attractions are open no matter the season.

Best Time to Visit: Provo Beach is open Monday through Thursday from 3:00 p.m. to 9:00 p.m. and Friday and Saturday from 11:00 a.m. to 10:00 p.m.

Pass/Permit/Fees: The fee to visit Provo Beach depends on the activity. It's $20 per hour for the FlowRider, $7 for laser tag, $8 for the ropes course, and $1.50 for the carousel. Bowling costs between $3 and $5 per game with an additional $2.50 for shoe rental. The playgrounds are $4 per child per day, and miniature croquet is $3 for children and $5 r adults.

Closest City or Town: Provo, Utah

Physical Address:
4801 N. University Avenue, Suite 210
Provo, UT 84604

GPS Coordinates: 40.30039° N, 111.65904° W

Did You Know? Provo Beach has been named the Best Family Fun Center in in the state by *Utah Valley Magazine* for 7 years in a row.

Provo Canyon Adventures

Want to view the Provo Canyon in a unique way? Try ziplining over the canopy and through the canyon at speeds of 40 miles per hour. Provo Canyon Adventures provides five zipline runs ranging from 300 feet to 1,100 feet, totaling about 1 mile of cable. Move from platform to platform as you take in the incredible views of the spectacular Provo landscape. From 1984 to 2011, the 1,280 acres of land was a ranch named Bear Canyon Ranch. Provo Canyon Adventures was meticulously designed to avoid disturbing the natural landscape, so when you fly over the canyon and canopy, you're seeing the unspoiled land the way it was meant to be seen.

Best Time to Visit: Provo Canyon Adventures is open Monday through Saturday from 8:00 a.m. to 7:00 p.m.

Pass/Permit/Fees: The cost to visit depends on the package you choose. Check the website for details.

Closest City or Town: Provo, Utah

Physical Address:
Mile marker 15 off Highway 189
Provo, UT 84604

GPS Coordinates: 40.37764° N, 111.55495° W

Did You Know? Guided raft trips and paddleboard and kayak rentals are also available through Provo Canyon Adventures.

Provo Canyon Scenic Byway

The Provo Canyon Scenic Byway takes drivers through the majestic Provo Canyon, past Deer Creek Reservoir and Bridal Veil Falls, and into the picturesque Heber Valley. The byway parallels the Provo River, which is one of the top fly-fishing rivers in Utah. There are numerous short side trips that are worth stopping for, including the Uinta National Forest, the Timpanogos Cave National Monument, and Sundance Resort. Careful observers might be able to spot mountain goats on the high cliffs, but you might need binoculars, as some of the cliffs are extremely tall. The byway is 32 miles long and takes about an hour to drive if you don't make any stops.

Best Time to Visit: This road stays open all year, but to see some incredible scenery with gorgeous colors, fall is the best time to visit.

Pass/Permit/Fees: There is no fee to drive the byway.

Closest City or Town: Provo, Utah

Physical Address:
Provo/Utah Valley Visitor's Center
220 W. Center Street
Provo, UT 84601

GPS Coordinates: 40.34012° N, 111.63395° W

Did You Know? From the western terminus in Olmstead, Bridal Veil Falls is a mere 4 miles into the Provo Canyon Scenic Byway drive, so if you don't have time to drive the entire byway, at least take some time to view this amazing waterfall.

Provo Pioneer Village

Provo Pioneer Village offers visitors an authentic pioneer trip back in time to 1849. Not only are there original structures from this time, including a school, woodshop, granary, corn crib, outhouse, and more, but there are also blacksmith, ox shoeing, and other demonstrations. Children can participate in pioneer games and learn about various historical tools and other artifacts. Visitors will love the authentic Turner Cabin, Haws Cabin, Loveless Home, and mercantile general store. Handcrafted pioneer goods and candy are for sale in the general store.

Best Time to Visit: The Provo Pioneer Village is open between Memorial Day and Labor Day from 5:00 p.m. to 8:00 p.m. on Monday, Wednesday, and Friday and from 11:00 a.m. to 3:00 p.m. on Saturday. Private tours for groups of 12 or more are available in the off season by appointment only.

Pass/Permit/Fees: There is no fee to visit the Provo Pioneer Village, but donations are appreciated.

Closest City or Town: Provo, Utah

Physical Address:
600 N. 500 West
Provo, UT 84601

GPS Coordinates: 40.24254° N, 111.66683° W

Did You Know? The Loveless Home, which is the former residence of James Washington Loveless, is the most recent structure donated to the Provo Pioneer Village, having arrived in 2013.

Provo River Parkway Trail

The Provo River Parkway Trail begins at Utah Lake State Park and ends in Provo Canyon. It is a paved 15-mile trail that accommodates walkers, joggers, rollerbladers, horseback riders, and bicyclists. It winds its way through both city and county parks, residential areas, and commercial developments. While there are a couple of steep climbs, they are rather short, and the trail is relatively flat most of the way. At the northern end of the trail, hikers pass by the base of Bridal Veil Falls, which makes for a spectacular view and photographic opportunity. The trail also goes through Orem and Provo, and there are plenty of parking lots, restrooms, and trail access points along the way.

Best Time to Visit: The best time to visit the Provo River Parkway Trail is during the spring, summer, or fall.

Pass/Permit/Fees: There is no fee to visit the Provo River Parkway Trail.

Closest City or Town: Provo

Physical Address:
Utah Lake State Park
4400 W. Center Street
Provo, Utah 84601

GPS Coordinates: 40.28397° N, 111.65950° W

Did You Know? The parks that are along the Provo River Parkway Trail include Utah Lake State Park, Canyon Glen Park, Nun's Park, Vivian Park, Fort Utah Park, Paul Ream Wilderness Park, and Exchange Park.

Splash Summit Waterpark

Splash Summit Waterpark offers 15 different slides, pools, and attractions, including a 500,000-gallon wave pool, which makes it a favorite summertime activity to cool off in the desert heat. The Canyon River is a relaxing pool that offers a gentle float past waterfalls, bridges, and small drop-offs. Cascade Falls is full of activities centered around relaxation and includes a gorgeous waterfall to play in or soak behind. Slides at the waterpark include the Vortex, the Sky Breaker, Mudslide Gorge, the Boomerang, the Summit Plunge, and others. For younger visitors, Adventure Bay provides a shallow pool with gentle water sprays and a small slide.

Best Time to Visit: Splash Summit Waterpark is open between late May and early September (just after Labor Day) from 10:00 a.m. to 6:00 p.m. In July, the closing time is extended to 8:00 p.m.

Pass/Permit/Fees: Admission is $24.99 for adults, $17.99 for children under 48 inches, and $14.99 for seniors ages 65 and up. Parking is $7 per vehicle, and tube rental is $6 each.

Closest City or Town: Provo, Utah

Physical Address:
1330 E. 300 North
Provo, UT 84606

GPS Coordinates: 40.23784° N, 111.63641° W

Did You Know? Splash Summit Water Park is 26 acres in size.

The Covey Center for the Arts

At the Covey Center for the Arts, visitors will find four art galleries and a performing arts venue. The center is the performance home for the Utah Regional Ballet, the Utah Valley Symphony, the Utah Premiere Brass, and the Wasatch Chorale. The main performance hall holds 670 guests. The Brinton "Black Box" Theater is more intimate with a seating capacity of 100 and is typically used for plays and other smaller productions. The center was built in 2007 and underwent renovation in 2011. It hosts more than 200 events each year.

Best Time to Visit: The best time to visit the Covey Center for the Arts is when an event, show, or exhibit you want to see is on stage or in the galleries. Check the website for showtimes and dates.

Pass/Permit/Fees: Some activities at the Covey Center for the Arts are free, but the cost will vary based on event and seat selection. Check the website for pricing details.

Closest City or Town: Provo, Utah

Physical Address:
425 W. Center Street
Provo, UT 84601

GPS Coordinates: 40.23424° N, 111.66601° W

Did You Know? The Covey Center for the Arts is named for Sandra M. Covey, a Provo resident who was a noted philanthropist and art enthusiast. She was also the wife of noted author Stephen Covey.

Utah Lake State Park

Utah Lake State Park is located near the Provo Airport and boasts the largest freshwater lake in the state at 148 square miles. The park features various recreational activities like fishing, swimming, boating, jet skiing, sailing, camping, canoeing, kayaking, and paddleboarding. Anglers enjoy Utah Lake for its abundance of walleye, black bass, white bass, channel catfish, and several panfish species. There's a swimming beach available in an area where nonmotorized boats are not allowed to make sure it's safe. A visitor center in the park showcases Native American grinding stones and arrowheads, an 1890s swimming suit, a 1950s fishing net, and numerous historical photographs.

Best Time to Visit: The best time to visit Utah Lake State Park is in the summer.

Pass/Permit/Fees: There is a $15 day-use fee per vehicle to visit Utah Lake State Park.

Closest City or Town: Provo, Utah

Physical Address:
4400 W. Center Street
Provo, UT 84601

GPS Coordinates: 40.23781° N, 111.73617° W

Did You Know? The Utah Lake Winter Fish Fest takes place at Utah Lake State Park every January.

American Fork Canyon

The American Fork Canyon is an attraction in its own right is named for the American Fork River, which carved the canyon over millions of years and still runs through the bottom of it today. There are plenty of recreational activities available in American Fork Canyon, including hiking, biking, and horseback riding, and Tibble Fork Reservoir and Silver Lake Flats Reservoir are popular areas for fishing in the summer. Cross-country skiing, snowshoeing, backcountry skiing, and snowmobiling are also available, so you shouldn't restrict your visits to warm-weather months only. There are at least nine camping sites in American Fork Canyon with varying levels of amenities. You can also just take the Alpine Scenic Loop Backway for a relaxing, picturesque drive through the Wasatch Mountains.

Best Time to Visit: The canyon is open year-round.

Pass/Permit/Fees: There is a $6 fee per vehicle to visit American Fork Canyon. The pass is valid for 3 days.

Closest City or Town: Salt Lake City, Utah

Physical Address:
Timpanogos Cave National Monument Visitor Center
1025 E. Alpine Drive
Alpine, UT 84004

GPS Coordinates: 40.43663° N, 111.73943° W

Did You Know? The first mine established in American Fork Canyon was the Pittsburgh Mine in 1870. It was discovered by soldiers stationed at Fort Douglas.

Beehive House

Located near the Mormon Temple and Temple Square in Salt Lake City, the Beehive House was once the residence of Brigham Young, president of The Church of Jesus Christ of Latter-Day Saints. He lived there from 1855 until he passed away in 1877. In his Beehive House and adjoining office, Young performed his duties as President of the LDS, territorial governor, and superintendent of Indian Affairs. Following his death, members of Young's family lived in the house until 1893. The house was eventually purchased by the LDS in 1898 and served as the official residence of Lorenzo Snow and Joseph F. Smith, two additional LDS presidents. Today, the Beehive House is a museum that tells the story of Brigham Young and its subsequent residents.

Best Time to Visit: The Beehive House is open Monday through Saturday from 10:00 a.m. to 2:00 p.m.

Pass/Permit/Fees: There is no fee to visit.

Closest City or Town: Salt Lake City, Utah

Physical Address:
67 E. South Temple Street
Salt Lake City, UT 84150

GPS Coordinates: 40.77060° N, 111.88849° W

Did You Know? After Joseph F. Smith passed away and until the 1950s, the Beehive House served as a boarding house for young women who were living in Salt Lake City for education or work.

Blackridge Reservoir

Blackridge Reservoir is a relatively small reservoir located in Herriman. It has a sandy beach that is open for swimming and picnicking, and visitors can paddleboard, kayak, canoe, or participate in other water sports on the reservoir itself. There is a small boat ramp located on the east side of the beach that is free for the public to use. It is ideal for a family getaway, as it features numerous amenities such as restrooms, concession stands, gazebos, picnic tables, and a playground. Blackridge Reservoir can sometimes be closed to swimming because of algae growth. Call before you visit.

Best Time to Visit: The best time to visit Blackridge Reservoir is between spring and fall but note that it is extremely crowded on summer holidays.

Pass/Permit/Fees: There is no fee to visit Blackridge Reservoir.

Closest City or Town: Salt Lake City, Utah

Physical Address:
15000 S. Ashland Ridge Drive
Herriman, UT 84096

GPS Coordinates: 40.48027° N, 112.02121° W

Did You Know? While this body of water was once open to fishermen, it has been closed to fishing since 2014.

Bridger Bay Beach

Bridger Bay Beach is located in Antelope Island State Park and is the best place to go swimming at the Great Salt Lake. The beach is very close to the shoreline (just 550 yards), and it is shallow enough to wade in before becoming a bit deeper for swimming. The Great Salt Lake is the largest saltwater lake in the Western Hemisphere, spanning approximately 1,700 square miles. There are no rivers exiting the Great Salt Lake, which contributes to its salinity because water must evaporate rather than flow elsewhere. There are also showers available to wash the saltwater off after swimming, and if you're hungry, there's the Island Buffalo Grill nearby.

Best Time to Visit: The best time to visit Bridger Bay Beach is in the summer.

Pass/Permit/Fees: There is a $10 fee per vehicle to visit Bridger Bay Beach.

Closest City or Town: Salt Lake City, Utah

Physical Address:
4528 W. 1700 South
Syracuse, UT 84075

GPS Coordinates: 41.04994° N, 112.25464° W

Did You Know? Bridger Bay Beach is named for Jim Bridger, the first white man to see the Great Salt Lake in 1824.

City Creek Center

City Creek Center is an upscale shopping center, residential area, and office space that features natural elements like foliage-lined walkways, an indoor/outdoor stream, a fountain, and other beautiful design features. The center opened to the public in 2012 and continues to be the destination of choice for shoppers looking for a wide range of luxury and chain stores. The main mall features an open-air design and award-winning retractable roof. A pedestrian skyway called the Skybridge connects the two upper floors of the mall across Main Street. Its design elements include roof panels that can be opened, interior benches, and glass walls.

Best Time to Visit: City Creek Center is open Monday through Wednesday from 11:00 a.m. to 7:00 p.m. and Thursday through Saturday from 11:00 a.m. to 8:00 p.m.

Pass/Permit/Fees: There is no fee to visit.

Closest City or Town: Salt Lake City, Utah

Physical Address:
50 S. Main Street
Salt Lake City, UT 84101

GPS Coordinates: 40.76905° N, 111.89126° W

Did You Know? The America First Credit Union Fountain at City Creek Center offers hourly shows and two feature shows at 7:00 p.m. and 9:00 p.m.

Hogle Zoo

Established in 1931, Utah's Hogle Zoo is located at the mouth of Emigration Canyon and encompasses more than 42 acres. Its unique position on the hillside with its abundance of trees gives Hogle Zoo a natural environment for housing hundreds of animals, including giraffes, ostriches, zebras, polar bears, river otters, and sea lions. Take the Zoofari Express train through many exhibits, or the Conservation Carousel is available to be enjoyed by visitors of all ages. Each animal on the carousel is hand carved and painted by an expert craftsman. There is an additional cost of $2.50 to ride the carousel.

Best Time to Visit: The Hogle Zoo is open daily from 9:00 a.m. to 6:00 p.m. from March 1 through October 31 and 10:00 a.m. to 5:00 p.m. from November 1 through February 28.

Pass/Permit/Fees: Admission to visit the Hogle Zoo is $19.95 for adults, $15.95 for children ages 3 to 12, and free for children ages 2 and under.

Closest City or Town: Salt Lake City, Utah

Physical Address:
2600 Sunnyside Avenue
Salt Lake City, UT 84108

GPS Coordinates: 40.75073° N, 111.81402° W

Did You Know? Up-close adventures such as giraffe experiences and elephant and rhino feedings are available at the Hogle Zoo for an extra cost.

Joseph Smith Memorial Building

The Joseph Smith Memorial Building is a 10-story multipurpose administrative building and social center located near the Mormon Temple in Salt Lake City. There is a 500-seat theater; three restaurants (The Roof Restaurant, The Nauvoo Café, and The Garden Restaurant); 13 large meeting and banquet rooms; and a full-service floral department (Flowers Squared) all available for rent. The theater also hosts a number of film screenings produced by The Church of Jesus Christ of Latter-Day Saints. The building was originally the Hotel Utah and was completed in 1911. It operated as a hotel until 1987, hosting guests from all over the world and in fields such as art, music, entertainment, and sports. The LDS church acquired the building and reopened it in 1993 as a meeting space and rental venue.

Best Time to Visit: The Joseph Smith Memorial Building is open Monday through Saturday from 9:00 a.m. to 9:00 p.m.

Pass/Permit/Fees: There is no fee to visit.

Closest City or Town: Salt Lake City, Utah

Physical Address:
15 E. South Temple Street
Salt Lake City, UT 84150

GPS Coordinates: 40.77064° N, 111.89038° W

Did You Know? The chapel located inside the Joseph Smith Memorial Building has a Casavant Freres pipe organ that has 2,484 pipes.

Liberty Park

This city park is the oldest and second largest in Salt Lake City. It features running/walking paths, tennis courts, a swimming pool, paddle boats, a playground, a children's amusement park, picnic facilities, and space for numerous community events. Prior to being used as a park, Liberty Park was a grist mill and farm, and it is still home to the oldest commercial building (the Isaac Chase Mill) in existence in Utah. The Chase Mill and Farm is well known for providing free grist to pioneers during the famine of 1857. In 1860, Brigham Young acquired the land and planted numerous trees, including mulberries and cottonwoods. He willed the land to the city upon his death so that it could be enjoyed by the public.

Best Time to Visit: The best time to visit Liberty Park is during the spring or fall, or when there is a community event that you want to attend. Check the website for dates and times.

Pass/Permit/Fees: There is no fee to visit Liberty Park.

Closest City or Town: Salt Lake City, Utah

Physical Address:
600 900 S
Salt Lake City, UT 84105

GPS Coordinates: 40.74479° N, 111.87412° W

Did You Know? Liberty Park is home to the Tracy Aviary, the oldest and largest free-standing aviary in the country.

Mormon Tabernacle

The Mormon Tabernacle was constructed in the 1800s to hold meetings for The Church of Jesus Christ of Latter-Day Saints. Until 2000, it was where the church held its biannual general conference, but the meeting grew too large for the facility and is now held at the LDS Conference Center. The Mormon Tabernacle is located on Temple Square and is still used for overflow crowds at the general conference. Construction began on the Mormon Tabernacle in 1863, finished in 1875, and is modeled after what was going to be the Canvas Tabernacle in Illinois. However, the Mormons left that state before it was ever built. The Mormon Tabernacle is home to the world-famous Mormon Tabernacle Choir and is acclaimed for its incredible acoustic qualities.

Best Time to Visit: The best time to visit the Mormon Tabernacle is when the Mormon Tabernacle Choir is performing. They hold public performances twice a week: Thursday from 8:00 p.m. to 9:30 p.m. and Sunday from 8:15 a.m. to 9:45 a.m.

Pass/Permit/Fees: There is no fee to visit.

Closest City or Town: Salt Lake City, Utah

Physical Address:
50 N. West Temple Street
Salt Lake City, UT 84150

GPS Coordinates: 40.77100° N, 111.89317° W

Did You Know? Since its opening, 12 U.S. presidents have given speeches from the Mormon Tabernacle pulpit.

Mormon Temple

As the largest temple of the Church of Jesus Christ of Latter-Day Saints, the Mormon Temple in Salt Lake City is 253,015 square feet in size and is the world headquarters of the Mormon religion. It was the sixth temple to be built and required 40 years to complete. It was the fourth temple constructed following the Mormon exodus from Illinois in 1846. There are no public tours of the temple, as a "temple recommend" is required to enter the building. However, the grounds are open to the public. The foundation was originally made from sandstone, but when several foundation stones cracked during the Utah War in the 1850s, the sandstone was replaced with a stronger rock. The walls are made from quartz monzonite, which was initially carried from Little Cottonwood Canyon by oxen and then by rail after 1869.

Best Time to Visit: The best times to visit the temple grounds are during the spring and summer when the gardens are in bloom.

Pass/Permit/Fees: There is no fee to visit the Mormon Temple grounds.

Closest City or Town: Salt Lake City, Utah

Physical Address:
50 N. West Temple Street
Salt Lake City, UT 84150

GPS Coordinates: 40.77044° N, 111.89180° W

Did You Know? There are numerous fascinating symbols in the architecture of the Mormon Temple.

Natural History Museum of Utah

Located in Salt Lake City, the Natural History Museum was first conceived in 1959 by a University of Utah faculty committee that wanted to consolidate several natural history collections from around the campus. The collection became the Utah Museum of Natural History in 1963 and was located on the University of Utah campus in the former George Thomas Library. In the 1960s, the museum's collection grew quickly with the discovery of tens of thousands of dinosaur bones in the Cleveland-Lloyd Dinosaur Quarry. The Natural History Museum of Utah now boasts over 1.6 million collection artifacts that are used for education and research.

Best Time to Visit: The Natural History Museum of Utah is open daily from 10:00 a.m. to 5:00 p.m. with an extending closing time of 9:00 p.m. on Wednesday.

Pass/Permit/Fees: Admission to the Natural History Museum of Utah is $19.95 for adults, $17.95 for young adults ages 13 to 24, and $14.95 for children ages 3 to 12. Children ages 2 and under are free.

Closest City or Town: Salt Lake City, Utah

Physical Address:
301 Wakara Way
Salt Lake City, UT 84108

GPS Coordinates: 40.76538° N, 111.82314° W

Did You Know? The Natural History Museum of Utah's building is wrapped in seam copper that was mined from Kennecott Utah Copper's Bingham Canyon Mine.

Salt Lake City Canyons

Salt Lake City is surrounded by mountains that are bisected by steep canyons. Parleys Canyon, located on the east side of the valley, is the most traveled due to I-80. Millcreek Canyon offers extensive hiking trails and is a popular spot for snowshoeing and cross-country skiing in the winter. There are several ski resorts throughout the area. Butterfield Canyon is southwest of Salt Lake City. It's a popular spot for biking, hiking, and horseback riding. Nearby Bingham Canyon leads to the world's largest open-pit copper mines. You can visit all seven canyons in any order, and information for Big Cottonwood Canyon is available below to help you get started.

Best Time to Visit: The best time to visit the canyons near Salt Lake City is between September and November.

Pass/Permit/Fees: There is no fee to visit the canyons near Salt Lake City.

Closest City or Town: Salt Lake City, Utah

Physical Address:
Visit Salt Lake
90 S W Temple Street
Salt Lake City, UT 84101

GPS Coordinates: 40.6373° N, 111.6330° W

Did You Know? In 1847, pioneers established this city under the name "Great Salt Lake City," which remained the official name until 1868.

Temple Square

Located in downtown Salt Lake City, Temple Square is a major center of history and religious activity for the Church of Jesus Christ of Latter-Day Saints, otherwise referred to as the Mormon religion. Temple Square encompasses five city blocks and features historic sites, fascinating exhibits, and family-oriented activities. All attractions in the square are geared to fulfill the church's mission. The Salt Lake Temple was conceived by Church President Brigham Young in 1847 and built in 1893 as a sacred place to worship God and Jesus Christ. The temple is also a geographical reference point, as all Salt Lake City streets are labeled according to their direction and distance from the Temple Square. Many free public events are held at Temple Square, but the architecture and gardens are always available for visiting.

Best Time to Visit: The best time to visit Temple Square is when there is a public event occurring. Check the website for dates and times.

Pass/Permit/Fees: All activities are free to the public.

Closest City or Town: Salt Lake City, Utah

Physical Address:
50 N. West Temple Street
Salt Lake City, UT 84150

GPS Coordinates: 40.77126° N, 111.89107° W

Did You Know? Every 2 years, Temple Square holds a 2-day gathering of its members that draws more than 80,000 people to the area.

This is the Place Heritage Park

A park that was truly built for everyone, This is the Place Heritage Park allows visitors to take a trip back in time to see the state as it was during its early settlement period. There are three trains to ride that take visitors on a tour of the park: the Blackhawk, the Jupiter, or the 119. You can also take the Mini Train that travels around the pond. Children can ride ponies, visit a petting farm, and even try their hand at milking a cow. The Treasure House provides an interactive mining experience. Guests can dig for gemstones at Prospector Pit, identify their treasures at the Assay Station, and pan for gold in the nearby creek, amongst many other activities.

Best Time to Visit: The park is open Monday through Saturday from 10:00 a.m. to 5:00 p.m.

Pass/Permit/Fees: In the winter season, admission is $7.95 for adults, $5.95 for children ages 3 to 11, and $6.95 for seniors ages 65 and up. In the summer season, admission is $14.95 for adults, $10.95 for children, and $13.95 for seniors.

Closest City or Town: Salt Lake City, Utah

Physical Address:
2601 E. Sunnyside Avenue
Salt Lake City, UT 8410

GPS Coordinates: 40.75325° N, 111.81564° W

Did You Know? There are more than 50 historic structures and homes to explore at This is the Place Heritage Park.

Timpanogos Cave National Monument

Known for its colorful caverns, Timpanogos Cave National Monument is one of the most popular cave destinations in Utah. The attraction is located in American Fork Canyon and can only be reached by hiking a 1.5-mile-long trail that, while paved, is fairly steep, climbing 1,160 feet in elevation. After the cave tour, you'll return to the Visitor Center by hiking down the same trail you came in on. This cave system is truly unique among those in the U.S. due to its abundance of cave formations.

Best Time to Visit: Tours of the caves are only available in the spring, summer, and fall.

Pass/Permit/Fees: Admission for the regular Cave Tour at the Timpanogos Cave National Monument is $12 for adults, $7 for children ages 2 to 11, and $2 for infants ages 1 and under. The Introduction to Caving Tour is limited to visitors ages 14 and older and costs $22 per person. Park fee is *not* required if you're only visiting the caves.

Closest City or Town: Salt Lake City, Utah

Physical Address:
2038 Alpine Loop Road
American Fork, UT 84003

GPS Coordinates: 40.44095° N, 111.70906° W

Did You Know? At the entrance of the caves, there are tiny fossilized coral and shells embedded in the limestone.

Tracy Aviary

Tracy Aviary one of two free-standing aviaries in the country. Over its 80-year history, the Tracy Aviary has grown to become a cultural landmark that provides educational programs to more than 60,000 children each year through camps, classes, and hands-on exhibits.

It is home to over 400 individual birds from 135 species and has been the site of numerous recovery efforts, including one for the trumpeter swan. Interactive experiences are always available to guests, including bird feedings and zookeeper shadowing. In addition to the educational opportunities available at the Tracy Aviary, the facility also focuses on conservation. In 2011, it founded the Conservation Science Program to protect local wild birds and their habitats in Utah.

Best Time to Visit: The Tracy Aviary is open daily from 9:00 a.m. to 5:00 p.m.

Pass/Permit/Fees: Admission is $11.95 for adults and $7.95 for children.

Closest City or Town: Salt Lake City, Utah

Physical Address:
589 E. 1300 S
Salt Lake City, UT 84105

GPS Coordinates: 40.74375° N, 111.87551° W

Did You Know? The Tracy Aviary includes a botanical garden with plants native to Utah that provide habitat for birds and other wildlife.

Utah State Capitol

As one of Utah's most prominent landmarks, the Utah State Capitol has become a popular tourist destination. Despite Utah being admitted as a state in 1896, construction didn't begin on the capitol until 1912 following several funding rejections and numerous design changes. Eventually, the design by Richard Kletting was selected by a narrow margin, and a groundbreaking ceremony was held on December 19, 1912. It wasn't until February 1915 that the legislature could move into the partially finished building, which wasn't completed until a year and a half later. The capitol has undergone several renovations and alterations since then and was placed on the National Register of Historic Places in 1978. Its architecture is generally Classical in style, but it also has Corinthian details.

Best Time to Visit: The Utah State Capitol is open Monday through Thursday from 7:00 a.m. to 8:00 p.m. and Friday through Sunday from 7:00 a.m. to 6:00 p.m.

Pass/Permit/Fees: There is no fee to visit the capitol.

Closest City or Town: Salt Lake City, Utah

Physical Address:
350 State Street
Salt Lake City, UT 84103

GPS Coordinates: 40.77809° W, 111.88822° W

Did You Know? The original capitol of Utah was supposed to be in Fillmore, but only the south wing was completed before the city ran out of money.

Angels Landing

Another popular destination in Zion National Park, Angels Landing is a rock formation that provides spectacular views of the 270-million-year-old Zion Canyon. The hike to the top of Angels Landing is not physically challenging, but it is mentally difficult as there are 21 steep switchbacks known as Walter's Wiggles and several sheer cliff drop-offs. People with a severe fear of heights should avoid this hike, even though there are chain railings. Because Angels Landing is so popular, the National Park Service has decided to issue permits to hike the trail through a seasonal lottery and a day-before lottery. You can enter both lotteries online.

Best Time to Visit: Visit during the spring or summer in the early morning or late afternoon.

Pass/Permit/Fees: There is a $25 fee per vehicle to enter Zion National Park and a $6 fee per person to enter the lotteries. People who win a hiking spot must pay an additional $3 fee.

Closest City or Town: Springdale, Utah

Physical Address:
Springdale Visitor Center
1101 Zion Park Boulevard
Springdale, UT 84767

GPS Coordinates: 37.27285° N, 112.94656° W

Did You Know? The "bucket list" hike to the summit of Angels Landing is considered one of the scariest hikes in America.

Grafton Ghost Town

For an inside look at a pioneer Mormon settlement, visit Grafton Ghost Town. Grafton was initially established by a small group of people who broke away from nearby Virgin. Residents started to leave Grafton in 1907, migrating to the larger town of Rockville where there were more opportunities. However, the last residents of Grafton didn't leave until 1944. Life in Grafton was not easy, even though the soil was fertile for crops of alfalfa, cotton, and wheat. There was the constant threat of floods, attacks by Native Americans, and harsh weather, particularly in the winter. Despite its proximity to Zion National Park (just a quarter of a mile away), Grafton is never crowded since it lies on the opposite side of the river. It's a quiet area that provides a lot of history in a small space.

Best Time to Visit: The best time to visit Grafton Ghost Town is during the spring, summer, or fall.

Pass/Permit/Fees: There is no fee to visit.

Closest City or Town: Springdale, Utah

Physical Address:
Springdale Visitor Center
1101 Zion Park Boulevard
Springdale, UT 84767

GPS Coordinates: 37.16826° N, 113.08179° W

Did You Know? The Grafton Ghost Town Cemetery is filled with as many as 84 graves, which is an indication of how difficult life was in the little settlement.

The Narrows

Located in Zion Canyon, The Narrows is the name for the narrowest part of the canyon. At some points, the gorge shrinks to just 20 feet wide with the towering, 1,000-foot walls looming above on both sides. There is a 1-mile wheelchair-accessible path called the Riverside Walk that will lead you to a viewing spot on The Narrows that starts at the Temple of Sinawava. You can also wade in the Virgin River. You must get your feet wet if you want to hike The Narrows, as there is no trail that goes through this part of the canyon. While the river is relatively shallow at most points, the area is also susceptible to flash flooding, so hiking The Narrows should be done with extreme caution.

Best Time to Visit: Visit in the late spring or summer when the water will be at its warmest and shallowest.

Pass/Permit/Fees: There is a $25 fee per vehicle, per week to visit The Narrows in Zion National Park.

Closest City or Town: Springdale, Utah

Physical Address:
Springdale Visitor Center
1101 Zion Park Boulevard
Springdale, UT 84767

GPS Coordinates: 37.30829° N, 112.94942° W

Did You Know? The Narrows, which follows the Virgin River, is the most popular hike in Zion National Park and is considered among the top slot-canyon hikes in the entire world.

Zion National Park

Zion Canyon offers panoramic views of steep red cliffs made from rock that is around 270 million years old. The photogenic area also contains diverse terrain and hiking options for all skill levels. Observation Point is an 8-mile trail to a summit offering a spectacular view of nearly every major attraction in the canyon. Angels Landing is strenuous, requiring the use of chains bolted into the cliffs. Emerald Pools is also a favorite, featuring a series of desert oases full of waterfalls, lush vegetation, and red-rock monoliths. You can tour the scenic drive via shuttle bus. It begins President's Day weekend and continues on the weekends until daily service begins in March. Private vehicles aren't permitted when the shuttle is in service.

Best Time to Visit: The best times to visit Zion National Park are in the spring and fall.

Pass/Permit/Fees: There is an entry fee of $35 per vehicle, $30 per motorcycle, or $20 per pedestrian to visit Zion National Park, all valid for 7 days. Shuttle tickets are $1 and must be purchased online in advance. A wilderness permit is required for overnight backpacking, canyoneering, climbing, narrows, and subway.

Closest City or Town: Springdale, Utah

Physical Address:
1 Zion Park Boulevard
State Route 9
Springdale, UT 84767

GPS Coordinates: 37.2982° N, 113.0263° W
Did You Know? Zion was the first national park in Utah.

Snow Canyon State Park

A 7,400-acre scenic park located in the Red Cliff Desert Reserve, Snow Canyon State Park is full of strikingly colorful majestic views. The area is surrounded by ancient lava flows and red Navajo sandstone, offering stunning red-rock vistas. The park's distinctive landscapes were shaped by lava flows and sand as recently as 27,000 years ago. You can explore the sandstone cliffs, petrified sand dunes, and lava fields of this terrain. With more than 38 miles of hiking trails, a 3-mile paved trail for walking and biking, and 15 miles of equestrian trails, there are plenty of areas to explore on this adventure.

Best Time to Visit: The best times to visit Snow Canyon State Park are in the spring and fall.

Pass/Permit/Fees: There is an entry fee of $10 per vehicle or $5 per group of pedestrians/cyclists (up to eight people) to visit Snow Canyon State Park.

Closest City or Town: St. George, Utah

Physical Address:
1002 Snow Canyon Drive
Ivins, UT 84738

GPS Coordinates: 37.2178° N, 113.6396° W

Did You Know? Contrary to its name, this park seldom receives snow. It was named after early Utah leaders Lorenzo and Erastus Snow.

St. George

Located partly in the Mojave Desert, partly on the Colorado Plateau, and partly in the Great Basin, St. George is a popular destination for outdoor enthusiasts. With mild weather throughout the year, there is always something to do, whether it's golfing, shopping, hiking, horseback riding, fishing, or visiting galleries and theaters. It is specifically known for its proximity to Zion National Park, but it is also close to Bryce Canyon and Capitol Reef, which makes it an excellent middle ground for adventurers of all types. Originally the home of the Hopi, Zuni, Pueblo, and Southern Paiute Native Americans, St. George was founded by Europeans in 1776 when the Dominguez-Escalante Expedition traveled through the area and settled with 300 Mormon families who arrived in 1861.

Best Time to Visit: St. George is pleasant to visit year-round.

Pass/Permit/Fees: There is no fee to visit St. George.

Closest City or Town: St. George, Utah

Physical Address:
Utah Welcome Center
1835 S. Convention Center Drive
St. George, UT 84790

GPS Coordinates: 37.07829° N, 113.58345° W

Did You Know? St. George was originally known as "Dixie" by Brigham Youngbecause it was founded as a cotton mission.

117

Capitol Reef National Park

Originally called "Wayne Wonderland" after its partial location in Wayne County, Capitol Reef National Park became a national monument in 1937. However, it was not opened to the public until 1950. The 100-mile rock formation called the Waterpocket Fold, which extends from Thousand Lake Mountain to Lake Powell, is preserved within the park. Capitol Reef is a specific point along the Waterpocket Fold that is known for its spectacular scenery. The first part of the park's name comes from the white Navajo Sandstone cliffs that have dome formations resembling those on many capitol buildings. The *reef* part of the name comes from the term for any rocky barrier to travel.

Best Time to Visit: The best times to visit Capitol Reef National Park are in the spring and fall when the weather is mild.

Pass/Permit/Fees: There is a $20 fee per vehicle to visit Capitol Reef National Park. The pass is valid for 7 days.

Closest City or Town: Torrey, Utah

Physical Address:
52 W. Headquarters Drive
Torrey, UT 84775

GPS Coordinates: 38.10200° N, -111.14071° W

Did You Know? The Waterpocket Fold located in Capitol Reef National Park was created by the same continental plates that created the Rocky Mountains.

Dinosaur National Monument

Most of Dinosaur National Monument is in Moffat County, Colorado. However, the Dinosaur Quarry portion of the park, the preservation of which was the primary reason for establishing the monument in 1915, is located in Utah. There are more than 800 paleontological sites in Dinosaur National Monument, boasting various fossils from Allosaurus, Abydosaurus, Deinonychus, and sauropod dinosaurs. The first fossils, which were eight Apatosaurs vertebra, were found in 1909 by paleontologist Earl Douglass. The Fremont Native American tribe lived in the Dinosaur National Monument area before the 14th century, and many artifacts of these people have also been found during archaeological digs.

Best Time to Visit: The best time to visit Dinosaur National Monument is between spring and fall, either in the morning or at dusk to see wildlife.

Pass/Permit/Fees: There is a $25 fee per vehicle to visit Dinosaur National Monument.

Closest City or Town: Vernal, Utah

Physical Address:
11625 E. 1500 South
Jensen, UT 84035

GPS Coordinates: 40.50969° N, 108.93396° W

Did You Know? Castle Park Archeological District and Mantle's Cave, two prehistoric locations within Dinosaur National Monument, have been placed on the National Register of Historic Places.

Red Fleet State Park

In the heart of dinosaur land, Red Fleet State Park provides recreation and a historical experience. Most of the park is dominated by the Red Fleet Reservoir, a 750-acre area that's great for boating, paddleboarding, kayaking, fishing, and swimming. Jumping from the sandstone cliffs surrounding the reservoir is also a popular, albeit dangerous, activity. There are also numerous hiking and biking trails in the area.

Dinosaur tracks have been preserved on the north shores of the reservoir. The area where the tracks are located is called Fossil Trackway. It can be accessed via the Dinosaur Trackway trail. Additionally, there is a campground at the reservoir if you'd like to explore for more than one day. Dinosaur National Monument is nearby, and Red Fleet is an International Dark Sky Park.

Best Time to Visit: Red Fleet State Park is great to visit any time of the year.

Pass/Permit/Fees: There is a $10 day-use fee to visit Red Fleet State Park.

Closest City or Town: Vernal, Utah

Physical Address:
8750 N. Highway 191
Vernal, UT 84078

GPS Coordinates: 40.5802° N, 109.4322° W

Did You Know? The dinosaur tracks are 200 million years old.

Uinta Mountains and Mirror Lake Highway

This part of Utah is designated as a roadless wilderness, vehicles are prohibited in most of the area. Much of the high, pristine mountain range is contained within Ashley National Forest. There is a famous scenic drive that is considered among the most beautiful in the country. State Route 150, also known as Mirror Lake Scenic Byway, stretches over 70 miles and passes the picturesque Mirror Lake as it traverses into the Uinta Mountains. Scenic viewpoints and numerous campgrounds are available along this high mountain road. The byway reaches an elevation of 10,687 feet at Bald Mountain Pass.

Best Time to Visit: The best time to visit the Uinta Mountains and Mirror Lake Highway is between June and early October, unless snowmobiling.

Pass/Permit/Fees: The fee to visit the Uinta Mountains and Mirror Lake Highway is $6 for 3 days or $12 for 7 days.

Closest City or Town: Vernal, Utah

Physical Address:
Rock Cliff Nature Center
2500 UT-32
Kamas, UT 84036

GPS Coordinates: 40.8827° N, 109.2971° W

Did You Know? The Uinta Mountain Range is an east–west chain of mountains.

Bonneville Salt Flats

Located in northwestern Utah, the densely packed salt pan named the Bonneville Salt Flats is one of the most unique natural features of the state. Stretching over 30,000 acres, the salt flats were formed when the ancient Lake Bonneville dried up. The salt levels vary in different areas.

The famous Bonneville Speedway is in the western portion. It looks like a frozen lakebed covered with snow. Other areas of the flats feature low mountains and hills where vegetation is sparse. An impressive spot to view the Salt Flats is an established rest stop along I-80. Views of the mountains to the north and west break up the land, while looking to the east and south makes it seem like the flat land extends forever.

Best Time to Visit: The best times to visit the Bonneville Salt Flats are during the summer and fall for dry conditions.

Pass/Permit/Fees: There is no fee to visit the Bonneville Salt Flats.

Closest City or Town: Wendover, Utah

Physical Address:
2370 S. Decker Lake Boulevard
West Valley City, UT 84119

GPS Coordinates: 40.7787° N, 113.8352° W

Did You Know? Lake Bonneville formed during the late Ice Age and covered nearly two-thirds of Utah.

Willard Bay

Willard Bay is a 9,900-acre reservoir located in Willard Bay State Park. It was once a part of the Great Salt Lake in Salt Lake City, but it was separated from it in 1964. Since then, it has been a source of irrigation water and recreation for the Wasatch Front metro area. It is especially popular with fishermen. The reservoir was created by the Arthur V. Watkins Dam, which was completed in 1964 to store surplus water from the Weber and Ogden Rivers so that it could be funneled to surrounding farmland. Today, Willard Bay visitors enjoy water skiing, boating, and swimming on the water. Willard Bay State Park, located on the eastern shore of Willard Bay, offers wildlife observation, hiking, and camping.

Best Time to Visit: The best time to visit Willard Bay is during the summer.

Pass/Permit/Fees: There is a $10 day-use fee per vehicle to visit Willard Bay.

Closest City or Town: Willard, Utah

Physical Address:
900 W. 650 North
Willard, UT 84340

GPS Coordinates: 41.38500° N, 112. 20432° W

Did You Know? Once Willard Bay was separated from the Great Salt Lake, it was drained of saltwater and refilled with freshwater. It is named for LDS apostle Willard Richards.

Proper Planning

With this guide, you are well on your way to properly planning a marvelous adventure. When you plan your travels, you should become familiar with the area, save any maps to your phone for access without internet, and bring plenty of water—especially during the summer months. Depending on which adventure you choose, you will also want to bring snacks or even a lunch. For younger children, you should do your research and find destinations that best suit your family's needs. You should also plan when and where to get gas, local lodgings, and food. We've done our best to group these destinations based on nearby towns and cities to help make planning easier.

Dangerous Wildlife

There are several dangerous animals and insects you may encounter while hiking. With a good dose of caution and awareness, you can explore safely. Here are steps you can take to keep yourself and your loved ones safe from dangerous flora and fauna while exploring:

- Keep to the established trails.
- Do not look under rocks, leaves, or sticks.
- Keep hands and feet out of small crawl spaces, bushes, covered areas, or crevices.
- Wear long sleeves and pants to keep arms and legs protected.
- Keep your distance should you encounter any dangerous wildlife or plants.

Limited Cell Service

Do not rely on cell service for navigation or emergencies. Always have a map with you and let someone know where you are and how long you intend to be gone, just in case.

First Aid Information

Always travel with a first aid kit in case of emergencies.

Here are items you should be certain to include in your primary first aid kit:

- Nitrile gloves
- Blister care products
- Band-Aids in multiple sizes and waterproof type
- Ace wrap and athletic tape
- Alcohol wipes and antibiotic ointment
- Irrigation syringe
- Tweezers, nail clippers, trauma shears, safety pins
- Small zip-lock bags containing contaminated trash

It is recommended to also keep a secondary first aid kit, especially when hiking, for more serious injuries or medical emergencies. Items in this should include:

- Blood clotting sponges

- Sterile gauze pads
- Trauma pads
- Second-skin/burn treatment
- Triangular bandages/sling
- Butterfly strips
- Tincture of benzoin
- Medications (ibuprofen, acetaminophen, antihistamine, aspirin, etc.)
- Thermometer
- CPR mask
- Wilderness medicine handbook
- Antivenin

There is much more to explore, but this is a great start.

For information on all national parks, visit https://www.nps.gov/index.htm .

This site will give you information on up-to-date entrance fees and how to purchase a park pass for unlimited access to national and state parks. This site will also introduce you to all of the trails at each park.

Always check before you travel to destinations to make sure there are no closures. Some hiking trails close when there is heavy rain or snow in the area and other parks close parts of their land for the migration of wildlife. Attractions may change their hours or temporarily shut down for various reasons. Check the websites for the most up-to-date information.

Made in United States
Troutdale, OR
06/14/2024